Y

Hans Christian Andersen's Fairy Tales

**Life itself
is the most wonderful
fairy tale**

5

“Life itself is the most wonderful fairy tale.”

CONTENTS

THE MARSH KING'S DAUGHTER (1858)

The storks tell many, many stories to their young ones, all about the bogs and marshes. In general, each story is suited to the age and sense of the little storks. While the youngest ones are satisfied with, "Kribble-krabble, plurry-murry," and think it a very fine story, the older ones demand something with more sense to it, or at least something about the family.

Of the two oldest stories which have been handed down among the storks, we all know the one about Moses, who was put by his mother on the banks of the Nile, where a king's daughter found him. How well she brought him up, how he became a great man, and how no one knows where he lies buried, are things that we all have heard.

The other tale is not widely known, perhaps because it is almost a family story. This tale has been handed down from one mother stork to another for a thousand years, and each succeding storyteller has told it better and better, and now we shall tell it best of all.

The first pair of storks who told this tale and who themselves played a part in it, had their summer home on the roof of the Viking's wooden castle up by the Wild Marsh in Vendsyssel. If we must be precise about our knowledge, this is in the country of Hjorring, high up near Skagen in Jutland. There is still a big marsh there, which we can read about in the official reports of that district. It is said that the place once lay under the sea, but the land has risen somewhat and is now a wilderness extending for many a mile. One is surrounded on all sides by marshy meadows, quagmires, and peat bogs, overgrown by cloud berries and stunted trees. Dank mists almost always hang over the place, and about seventy years ago, wolves still made their homes there. Well may it be called the Wild Marsh. Think how desolate it was, and how much swamp and water there must have been among all those marshes and ponds a thousand years ago! Yet in most matters, it must have looked then as it looks now. The reeds grew just as high, and had the same long leaves and feathery tips of a purplish-brown tint that they have now. Birch trees grew there with the same white bark and the same airily dangling leaves. As for the living creatures, the flies have not changed the cut of their gauzy apparel, and the favorite colors of the storks were white trimmed with black, and long red stockings.

However, people dressed very differently from the fashion of today. But if any of them—thrall or huntsman, it mattered not—set foot in the quagmire, they fared the same a thousand years ago as they would fare today. In they would fall, and down they would sink to him whom they call the Marsh King, who rules below throughout the entire marsh land. They also call him King of the Quicksands, but we like the name Marsh King better, and that was what the storks called him. Little or nothing is known about his rule, but perhaps that is just as well.

Near the marsh and close to the Liim Fjord, lay wooden castle of the Vikings, three stories high from its watertight stone cellars to the tower on its roof. The storks had built their nest on this roof, and there the mother stork sat hatching her eggs. She was certain they would be hatched.

One evening, the father stork stayed out rather late, and when he got home, he looked ruffled and flurried.

"I have something simply dreadful to tell you," he said to the mother stork.

"Then you had better keep it to yourself," she told him. "Remember, I am hatching eggs! If you frighten me, it might have a very bad effect on them."

"But I must tell you," he insisted. "The daughter of our Egyptian host has come here. She has ventured to take this long journey, and—she's lost!"

"She who comes of fairy stock? Speak up. You know that I must not be kept in suspense while I'm on my eggs."

"It's this way, Mother. Just as you told me, she must have believed the doctor's advice. She believed that the swamp flowers up here would cure her sick father, and she has flown here in the guise of a swan, together with two other princesses who put on swan plumage and fly north every year, to take the baths that keep them young. She has come, and she is lost."

"You make your story too long-winded," the mother stork protested. "My eggs are apt to catch cold. I can't bear such suspense at a time like this."

"I have been keeping my eyes open," said the father stork, "and this evening I went among the reeds where the quagmire will barely support me. There I saw three swans flying my way. There was something about their flight that warned me, 'See here! These are not real swans. These creatures are merely disguised in swan feathers!' You know as well as I do, Mother, that one feels instinctly whether a thing is true or false."

"To be sure, I do," said she. "But tell me about the princess. I am tired of hearing about swan feathers."

"Well," the father stork said, "as you know, in the middle of the marsh, there is a sort of pool. You can catch a glimpse of it from here if you will rise up a trifle. There, between the reeds and the green scum of the pool, a large alder stump juts up. On it the three swans alighted, flapped their wings and looked about them. One of them threw off her swan plumage and immediately I could see that she was the princess from our home in Egypt. There she sat with no other cloak than her own long hair. I heard her ask the others to take good care of her swan feathers, while she dived down in the water to pluck the swamp flower which she fancied she saw there. They nodded, and held their heads high as they picked up her empty plumage.

"'What are they going to do with it?' I wondered, and she must have wondered, too. Our answer came soon enough, for they flew up in the air with her feather garment.

"'Dive away,' they cried. 'Never more shall you fly about as a swan. Never more shall you see the land of Egypt. You may have your swamp forever.' They tore her swan guise into a hundred pieces, so that feathers whirled around like a flurry of snow. Then away they flew, those two deceitful princesses."

"Why, that's dreadful," the mother stork said. "I can't bear to listen. Tell me what happened next."

"The princess sobbed and lamented. Her tears sprinkled down on the alder stump, and the stump moved, for it was the Marsh King himself, who lives under the quagmire. I saw the stump turn, and this was no longer a tree stump that stretched out its two muddy, branchlike arms toward the poor girl. She was so frightened that she jumped out on the green scum which cannot bear my weight, much less hers. She was instantly swallowed up, and it was the alder stump, which plunged in after her, that dragged her down. Big black bubbles rose, and these were the last traces of them. She is now buried in the Wild Marsh, and never will she get back home to Egypt with the flowers she came to find. Mother, you could not have endured the sights I saw."

"You ought not to tell me such a tale at a time like this. Our eggs may be the worse for it. The princess can look out for herself. Someone will surely help her. Now if it had been I, or you, or any of our family, it would have been all over with us."

"I shall look out for her, every day," said the father stork, and he did so.

A long time went by, but one day, he saw a green stalk shooting up from the bottom of the pool. When it came to the surface, it grew a leaf, which got broader and broader, and then a bud appeared. As the stork was flying by one morning, the bud opened in the strong sunbeams, and in the center of it lay a beautiful child, a baby girl who looked as fresh as if she had just come from her bath. So closely did the baby resemble the princess from Egypt that the stork thought it was she, who had become a child again. But when he considered the matter, he decided that this child who lay in the cup of a water lily must be the daughter of the princess and the Marsh King.

"She cannot remain there," the stork said to himself, "yet my nest is already overcrowded. But I have an idea. The Viking's wife hasn't any children, although she is always wishing for a little one. I'm often held responsible for bringing children, and this time I shall really bring one. I shall fly with this baby to the Viking's wife. What joy there will be."

The stork picked up the little girl, flew with her to the log castle, pecked a hole with his beak in the piece of bladder that served as a window pane, and laid the baby in the arms of the Viking woman. Then he flew home to his wife and told her all about it. The baby storks listened attentively, for they were old enough now to be curious.

"Just think! The princess is not dead," he told them. "She sent her little one up to me, and I have found a good home for it."

"I told you to start with that it would come out all right," said the mother stork. "Turn your thoughts now to your own children. It is almost time for us to start on our long journey. I am beginning to tingle under my wings. The cuckoo and the nightingale have flown already, and I heard the quail saying that we shall soon have a favorable wind. Our young ones will do us credit on the flight, or I don't know my own children."

How pleased the Viking's wife was when she awoke in the morning and found the lovely child in her arms. She kissed it and caressed it, but it screamed frightfully and thrashed about with its little arms and legs. There was no pleasing it until at last it cried itself to sleep, and as it lay there, it was one of the loveliest little creatures that anyone ever saw. The Viking's wife was so overjoyed that she felt light-headed as well as light-hearted. She turned quite hopeful about everything, and felt sure that her husband and all his men might return as unexpectedly as the little one had come to her. So she set herself and her entire household to work, in order to have everything in readiness. The long, colored tapestry on which she and her handmaidens had embroidered figures of their gods—Odin, Thor, and Freya, as they were called—were hung in place. The thralls were set to scouring and polishing the old shields that decorated the walls; cushions were laid on the benches; and dry logs were stacked on the fireplace in the middle of the hall, so that the pile might be lighted at a moment's notice. The Viking's wife worked so hard that she was tired out, and slept soundly when evening came.

Along toward morning she awoke, and was greatly alarmed to find no trace of her little child. She sprang up, lighted a splinter of pine wood, and searched the room. To her astonishment, she found at the foot of her bed not the beautiful child, but a big, ugly frog. She was so appalled that she took up a heavy stick to kill the creature, but it looked at her with such strange, sad eyes that she could not strike. As she renewed her search, the frog gave a faint, pitiful croak. She sprang from the bed to the window, and threw open the shutter. The light of the rising sun streamed in and fell upon that big frog on the bed. It seemed as if the creature's wide mouth contracted into small, red lips. The frog legs unbent as the most exquisitely shaped limbs, and it was her lovely little child that lay there, and not that ugly frog.

"What's all this?" she exclaimed. "Have I had a nightmare? This is my pretty little elf lying here." She kissed it and pressed it affectionately to her heart, but it struggled and tried to bite, like the kitten of a wild cat.

Neither that day nor the next did her Viking husband come home. Though he was on his way, the winds were against him. They were blowing southward to speed the storks. A fair wind for one is a foul wind for another.

In the course of a few days and nights, it became plain to the Viking's wife how things were with the little child. It was under the influence of some terrible spell of sorcery. By day it was as lovely as a fairy child, but it had a wicked temper. At night, on the contrary, it was an ugly frog, quiet and pathetic, with sorrowful eyes. Here were two natures that changed about both inwardly and outwardly. This was because the little girl whom the stork had brought had by day her mother's appearance, together with her father's temper. But at night, she showed her kinship with him in her outward form, while her mother's mind and heart inwardly became hers. Who would be able to release her from this powerful spell of sorcery that lay upon her? The Viking's wife felt most anxious and distressed about it, yet her heart went out to the poor little thing.

She knew that when her husband came home she would not dare tell him of this strange state of affairs, for he would certainly follow the custom of those times and expose the poor child on the high road, to let anyone take it who would. The Viking's good-natured wife had not the heart to do this, so she determined that he should only see the child in the daytime.

At daybreak one morning, the wings of storks were heard beating over the roof. During the night, more than a hundred pairs of storks had rested there, and now they flew up to make their way to the south.

"Every man ready," was their watchword. "Let the wives and children make ready, too."

"How light we feel!" clacked the little storks. "We tingle and itch right down to our toes, as if we were full of live frogs. How fine it feels to be traveling to far-off lands."

"Keep close in one flock," cried their father and mother. "Don't clack your beaks so much, it's bad for your chest."

And away they went.

At that very instant, the blast of a horn rang over the heath, to give notice that the Viking had landed with all of his men.

They came home with rich booty from the Gaelic coast, where, as in Britain, the terrified people sang, "Deliver us from the wild Northmen."

What a lively bustle now struck this Viking's castle near the Wild Marsh! A cask of mead was rolled out into the hall, the pile of wood was lighted, and horses were slaughtered. What a feast they were going to have! Priests sprinkled the horses' warm blood over the thralls as a blood offering. The fires crackled, the smoke rolled up to the roof, and soot dropped down from the beams, but they were used to that. Guests were invited and were given handsome presents. Old grudges and double-dealings were forgotten. They all drank deep and threw the gnawed bones in each other's faces, but that was a sign of good humor. The skald, a sort of minstrel but at the same time a fighting man who had been with them and knew what he sang about, trolled them a song, in which he told of all their valiant deeds in battle, and all their wonderful adventures. After each verse came the same refrain:

Fortunes perish, friends die, one dies oneself,
But a glorious name never dies!

Then they all banged their shields, and rattled on the table with their knives or the knucklebones, making a terrific noise.

The Viking's wife sat on the bench that ran across this public banquet hall. She wore a silken dress with gold bracelets and big amber beads. She was in her finest attire, and the skald included her in his song. He spoke of the golden treasure which she had brought her rich husband. This husband of hers rejoiced in the lovely child whom he had seen only by day, in all its charming beauty. The savage temper that went with her daytime beauty rather pleased him, and he said that she might grow up to be a stalwart soldier maid, able to hold her own—the sort who would not flinch if a skilled hand, in fun, took a sharp sword and cut off her eyebrows for practice.

The mead cask was emptied, a full one was rolled in, and it too was drunk dry. These were folk who could hold a great deal. They were familiar with the old proverb to the effect that, "The cattle know when to quit their pasture, but a fool never knows the measure of his stomach."

Yes, they all knew it quite well, but people often know the right thing and do the wrong thing. They also knew that, "One wears out his welcome when he sits too long in another man's house," but they stayed on, for all that. Meat and mead are such good things, and they were a jovial crew. That night the thralls slept on the warm ashes, dipped their fingers into the fat drippings, and licked them. Oh yes, those were glorious days.

The Vikings ventured forth on one more raid that year, though the storms of autumn were beginning to blow. The Viking and his men went to the coast of Britain—"just across the water," he said—and his wife stayed at home with her little girl. It soon came about that the foster mother cared more for the poor frog with its sad eyes and pathetic croaking, than for the little beauty who scratched and bit everyone who came near her.

The raw, dank mist of fall invaded the woods and thickets. "Gnaw-worms," they called it, for it gnawed the leaves from the trees. "Pluck-feathers," as they called the snow, fell in flurry upon flurry, for winter was closing in. Sparrows took over the stork nest and gossiped about the absent owners, as tenants will. The two storks and all their young ones—where were they now?

The storks were now in the land of Egypt, where the sun shone as warm as it does upon us on a fine summer day. Tamarind and acacia trees bloomed in profusion, and the glittering crescent of Mohammed topped the domes of all the mosques. On the slender minarets many a pair of storks rested after their long journey. Whole flocks of them nested together on the columns of ancient temples and the ruined arches of forgotten cities. The date palm lifted its high screen of branches, like a parasol in the sun. The gray-white pyramids were sharply outlined against the clear air of the desert, where the ostrich knew he could use his legs and the lion crouched to gaze with big solemn eyes at the marble sphinx half buried in the sand. The waters of the Nile had receded, and the delta was alive with frogs. The storks considered this the finest sight in all the land, and the young storks found it hard to believe their own eyes. Yes, everything was wonderful.

"See! It is always like this in our southern home," their mother told them. And their little bellies tingled at the spectacle.

"Do we see any more?" they asked. "Shall we travel on into the country?"

"There is nothing else worth seeing," their mother said. "Beyond this fertile delta lie the deep forests, where the trees are so interwoven by thorny creepers that only the elephant can trample a path through them with his huge, heavy feet. The snakes there are too big for us to eat, and the lizards too nimble for us to catch. And, if you go out in the desert, the slightest breeze will blow your eyes full of sand, while a storm would bury you under the dunes. No, it is best here, where there are plenty of frogs and locusts. Here I stop, and here you stay."

So they stayed. In nests atop the slender minarets the old storks rested, yet kept quite busy smoothing their feathers and sharpening their bills against their red stockings. From time to time, they would stretch their necks, bow very solemnly, and hold up their heads with such high foreheads, fine feathers, and wise brown eyes. The young maiden storks strolled solemnly through the wet reeds, making eyes at the other young storks and scraping acquaintances. At every third step they would gulp down a frog, or pause to dangle a small snake in their bills. They were under the impression that this became them immensely and besides, it tasted so good.

The young bachelor storks picked many a squabble, buffeted each other with their wings, and even stabbed at each other with their sharp bills till blood was shed. Yes, and then this young stork would get engaged, and that young stork would get engaged. Maidens and bachelors would pair off, for that was their only object in life. They built nests of their own and squabbled anew, for in the hot countries everyone is hotheaded. But it was very pleasant there, particularly so for the old storks, who thought that their children could do no wrong. The sun shone every day, there was plenty to eat, and they had nothing to do but enjoy themselves.

However, in the splendid palace of their Egyptian host, as they called him, there was no enjoyment. This wealthy and powerful lord lay on his couch, as stiff and stark as a mummy. In the great hall, which was as colorful as the inside of a tulip, he was surrounded by his kinsmen and servants. Though he was not quite dead, he could hardly be said to be alive. The healing flower from the northern marshes, which she who had loved him best had gone to seek, would never reach him. His lovely young daughter, who had flown over land and sea in the guise of a swan, would never come home from the far North.

"She is dead and gone," the two other swan princesses reported, when they returned. They concocted the following yarn, which they told:

"We three were flying together through the air, when a huntsman shot an arrow at us, and it struck our companion, our young friend. Like a dying swan, she sang her farewell song as she slowly dropped down to a lake in the forest. There on the shore we buried her, under a drooping birch tree. But we avenged her. We bound coals of fire to the wings of a swallow that nested under the thatched eaves of the huntsman's cottage. The roof blazed up, the cottage burst into flames, and the huntsman was burned to death. The flames were reflected across the lake, under the drooping birch tree where she lies, earth of this Earth. Never, alas! shall she return to the land of Egypt."

They both wept. But when the father stork heard their tale he rattled his bill, and said, "All lies and invention! I should dearly love to drive my bill right through their breasts."

"And most likely break it," said the mother stork. "A nice sight you'd be then. Think first of yourself, and then of your family. Never mind about outsiders."

"Nevertheless, I shall perch on the open cupola tomorrow, when all the wise and learned folk come to confer about the sick man. Perhaps they will hit upon something nearer the truth."

The wise men assembled and talked loud and long, but neither could the stork make sense out of what they had to say, nor did any good come of it to the sick man or to his daughter in the Wild Marsh. Yet we may as well hear what they had to say, for we have to listen to a lot in this world.

Perhaps it will be well to hear what had gone on before down there in Egypt. Then we shall know the whole story, or at least as much of it as the father stork knew.

"Love brings life. The greatest love brings the greatest life. Only through love may life be brought back to him." This doctrine the learned men had stated before, and they now said they had stated it wisely and well.

"It is a beautiful thought," the father stork quickly agreed.

"I don't quite understand it," said the mother stork. "That's its fault though, not mine. But no matter. I have other things to think about."

The learned men talked on about all the different kinds of love: the love of sweethearts, the love between parents and their children, plants' love of the light, and the love that makes seeds grow when the sun's rays kiss the earth. Their talk was so elaborate and learned that the father stork found it impossible to follow, much less repeat. However, their discussion made him quite thoughtful. All the next day he stood on one leg, with his eyes half closed, and thought, and thought. So much learning lay heavy upon him.

But one thing he understood clearly. Both the people of high degree and the humble folk had said from the bottom of their hearts that for this man to be sick, without hope of recovery, was a disaster to thousands, yes, to the whole nation, and that it would bring joy and happiness to everyone if he recovered.

"But where does the flower grow that can heal him?" they asked. For the answer they looked to their scholarly manuscripts, to the twinkling stars, to the wind, and to the weather. They searched through all the bypaths of knowledge, but all their wisdom and knowledge resolved down to the doctrine: "Love brings life—it can bring back a father's life," and although they said rather more than they understood, they accepted it, and wrote it down as a prescription. "Love brings life." Well and good, but how was this precept to be applied? That was their stumbling block.

However, they had at last agreed that help must come from the princess, who loved her father with all her heart. And they had devised a way in which she could help him. It was more than a year ago that they had sent the princess into the desert, just when the new moon was setting, to visit the marble sphinx. At the base of the sphinx she had to scrape away the sand from a doorway and follow a long passage which led to the middle of a great pyramid where one of the mightiest kings of old lay wrapped as a mummy in the midst of his glory and treasure. There she leaned over the corpse to have it revealed to her where she might find life and health for her father. When she had done all this, she had a dream in which she learned that in the Danes' land there was a deep marsh—the very spot was described to her. Here, beneath the water, she would feel a lotus flower touch her breast, and when that flower was brought home to her father it would cure him. So, in the guise of a swan she had flown from the land of Egypt to the Wild Marsh.

All this was known to the father and mother stork, and now we too are better informed. Furthermore, we know that the Marsh King dragged her down, and that those at home thought her dead and gone. Only the wisest among them said, as the stork mother had put it, "She can look out for herself." They waited to see what would come to pass, for they knew nothing better they could do.

"I believe I shall make off with those swan feathers of the faithless princesses," said the father stork. "Then they will fly no more to do mischief in the Wild Marsh. I'll hide the two sets of feathers up North, until we find a use for them."

"Where would you keep them?" the mother stork asked.

"In our nest by the Wild Marsh," he said. "I and our sons will take turns carrying them when we go back. If they prove too much of a burden, there are many places along the way where we can hide them until our next flight. One set of swan feathers would be enough for the princess, but two will be better. In that northern land it's well to have plenty of wraps."

"You will get no thanks for it," she told him, "but please yourself. You are the master, and except at hatching time, I have nothing to say."

Meanwhile, in the Viking's castle near the Wild Marsh, toward which the storks came flying, now that it was spring, the little girl had been given a name. She was called Helga, but this name was too mild for the violent temper that this lovely girl possessed. Month by month her temper grew worse. As the years went by and the storks traveled to and fro, to the banks of the Nile in the fall, and back to the Wild Marsh in the springtime, the child grew to be a big girl. Before anyone would have thought it, she was a lovely young lady of sixteen. The shell was fair to see but the kernel was rough and harsh—harsher than most, even in that wild and cruel age.

She took delight in splashing her hands about in the blood of horses slaughtered as an offering to the gods. In savage sport, she would bite off the head of the black cock that the priest was about to sacrifice, and in dead earnest she said to her foster father:

"If your foe were to come with ropes and pull down the roof over your head, I would not wake you if I could. I would not even hear the house fall, for my ears still tingle from that time you boxed them, years ago—yes, you! I'll never forget it."

But the Viking did not believe she was serious. Like everyone else, he was beguiled by her beauty, and he did not know the change that came over Helga's body and soul.

She would ride an unsaddled horse at full gallop, as though she were part of her steed, nor would she dismount even though he fought with his teeth against the other wild horses. And many a time she would dive off the cliff into the sea, with all of her clothes on, and swim out to meet the Viking as his boat neared home. To string her bow, she cut off the longest lock of her beautiful hair, and plaited it into a string. "Self-made is well made," said she.

The Viking's wife had a strong and determined will, in keeping with the age, but with her daughter she was weak and fearful, for she knew that an evil spell lay on that dreadful child.

Out of sheer malice, as it seemed, when Helga saw her foster mother stand on the balcony or come into the courtyard, she would sit on the edge of the well, throw up her hands, and let herself tumble into that deep, narrow hole. Froglike, she would dive in and clamber out. Like a wet cat, she would run to the main hall, dripping such a stream of water that the green leaves strewn on the floor were floating in it.

However, there was one thing that held Helga in check—and

that was evening. As she came on, she grew quiet and thoughtful. She would obey and accept advice. Some inner force seemed to make her more like her real mother. When the sun went down and the usual change took place in her appearance and character, she sat quiet and sad, shriveled up in the shape of a frog. Now that she had grown so much larger than a frog, the change was still more hideous. She looked like a miserable dwarf, with the head and webbed fingers of a frog. There was something so very pitiful in her eyes, and she had no voice. All she could utter was a hollow croak, like a child who sobs in her dreams. The Viking's wife would take this creature on her lap. Forgetting the ugly form as she looked into those sad eyes, she would often say, "I almost wish that you would never change from being my poor dumb-stricken frog child. For you are more frightful when I see you cloaked in beauty."

Then she would write out runes against illness and witchcraft and throw them over the wretched girl, but it was little good they did.

"One can hardly believe that she was once so tiny that she lay in the cup of a water lily," said the father stork. "She has grown up and is the living image of her Egyptian mother, whom we'll never see again. She did not look out for herself as well as you and those wise men predicted she would. Year in, year out, I've flown to and fro across the Wild Marsh, but never a sign have I seen of her. Yes, I may as well tell you that year after year, when I flew on ahead to make our nest ready and put things in order, I spent whole nights flying over the pool as if I were an owl or a bat, but to no avail. Nor have we found a use for the two sets of swan feathers, which I and our sons took so much trouble to bring all the way from the banks of the Nile. It took us three trips to get them here. For years now they have lain at the bottom of our nest. If perchance a fire broke out and this wooden castle burned down, they would be gone."

"And our good nest would be gone too," the mother stork reminded him. "But you care less for that than you do for your swan feathers and your swamp princess. Sometime you ought to go down in the mire with her and stay there for good. You are a poor father to your children, just as I've been telling you ever since I hatched our first brood. All I hope is that neither we nor our young ones get an arrow shot under our wings by that wild Viking brat. She doesn't know what she is doing. I wish she would realize that this has been our home much longer than it has been hers. We have always been punctilious about paying our rent every year with a feather, an egg, and a young one, according to custom. But do you think that, when she is around, I dare venture down into the yard, as I used to, and as I still do in Egypt, where I am everyone's crony and they let me peer into every pot and kettle? No, I sit up here vexing myself about her—the wench!—and about you, too. You should have left her in the water lily, and that would have been the end of her."

"You aren't as hardhearted as you sound," said the father stork. "I know you better than you know yourself." Up he hopped, twice he beat with his wings, and stretching his legs behind him, off he flew, sailing away without moving his wings until he had gone some distance. Then he took a powerful stroke. The sunlight gleamed on his white feathers. His neck and head were stretched forward. There were speed and swing in his flight.

"After all, he's the handsomest fellow of all," said the mother stork, "but you won't catch me telling him so."

Early that fall the Viking came home with his booty and captives. Among the prisoners was a young Christian priest, one of those who preached against the northern gods. Of late there had been much talk in hall and bower about the new faith that was spreading up from the south, and for which St. Ansgarius had won converts as far north as Hedeby on the Slie. Even young Helga had heard of this faith in the White Christ, who so loved mankind that he had given his life to save them. But as far as she was concerned, as the saying goes, such talk had come in one ear and gone out the other. Love was a meaningless word to her except during those hours when, behind closed doors, she sat shriveled up as a frog. But the Viking's wife had heard the talk, and she felt strangely moved by the stories that were told about the son of the one true God.

Back from their raid, the Vikings told about glorious temples of costly hewn stone, raised in honor of him whose message is one of love. They had brought home with them two massive vessels, artistically wrought in gold, and from these came the scent of strange spices. They were censers, which the Christian priests swung before altars where blood never flowed, but instead the bread and wine were changed into the body and blood of him who had given himself for generations yet unborn.

Bound hand and foot with strips of bark, the young priest was cast into the deep cellars of the Viking's castle. The Viking's wife said that he was as beautiful as the god Balder, and she was sorry for him, but young Helga proposed to have a cord drawn through his feet and tied to the tails of wild oxen.

"Then," she exclaimed, "I would loose the dogs on him. Ho, for the chase through mud and mire! That would be fun to see, and it would be even more fun to chase him."

But this was not the death that the Viking had in mind for this enemy and mocker of the high gods. Instead, he planned to sacrifice the priest on the blood stone in their grove. It would be the first human sacrifice that had ever been offered there.

Young Helga begged her father to let her sprinkle the blood of the victim upon the idols and over the people. When one of the many large, ferocious dogs that hung about the house came within reach while she was sharpening her gleaming knife, she buried the blade in his side, "Just to test its edge," she said.

The Viking's wife looked in distress at this savage, ill-natured girl, and when night came and the beauty of body and soul changed places in the daughter, the mother spoke of the deep sorrow that lay in her heart. The ugly frog with the body of a monster gazed up at her with its sad brown eyes. It seemed to listen, and to understand her as a human being would.

"Never once, even to my husband, have I let fall a word of the two-edged misery you have brought upon me," said the Viking's wife. "My heart is filled with more sorrow for you than I would have thought it could hold, so great is a mother's love. But love never entered into your feelings. Your heart is like a lump of mud, dank and cold. From whence came you into my house?"

The miserable form trembled strangely, as if these words had touched some hidden connection between its soul and it hideous body. Great tears came into those eyes.

"Your time of disaster will come," said the Viking's wife, "and it will be a disastrous time for me, too. Better would it have been to have exposed you beside the highway when you were young, and to have let the cold of the night lull you into the sleep of death." The Viking's wife wept bitter tears. In anger and distress, she passed between the curtains of hides that hung from a beam and divided the chamber.

The shriveled-up frog crouched in a corner. The dead quiet was broken at intervals by her half-stifled sighs. It was as if in pain a new life had been born in her heart. She took a step forward, listened, stepped forward again, and took hold of the heavy bar of the door with her awkward hands. Softly she unbarred the door. Silently she lifted the latch. She picked up the lamp that flickered in the hall outside, and it seemed that some great purpose had given her strength. She drew back the iron bolt from the well-secured cellar door, and stole down to the prisoner. He was sleeping as she touched him with her cold, clammy hand. When he awoke and saw the hideous monster beside him, he shuddered as if he had seen an evil specter. She drew her knife, severed his bonds, and beckoned for him to follow her.

He uttered holy names and made the sign of the Cross. As the creature remained unchanged, he said, in the words of the Bible:

"'Blessed is he that considereth the poor. The Lord will deliver him in time of trouble.' Who are you, that in guise of an animal are so gentle and merciful?"

The frog beckoned for him to follow her. She led him behind sheltering curtains and down a long passage to the stable, where she pointed to a horse. When he mounted it, she jumped up in front ot him, clinging fast to the horse's mane. The prisoner understood her, and speedily they rode out on the open heath by a path he could never have found.

He ignored her ugly shape, for he knew that the grace and kindness of God could take strange forms. When he prayed and sang hymns, she trembled. Was it the power of song and prayer that affected her, or was she shivering at the chill approach of dawn? What had come over her? She rose up, trying to stop the horse so that she could dismount, but the Christian priest held her with all his might, and chanted a psalm in the hope that it might have power to break the spell which held her in the shape of a hideous frog.

The horse dashed on, more wildly than ever. The skies turned red, and the first ray of the sun broke through the clouds. In that first flash of sunlight she changed. She became the lovely maiden with the cruel, fiendish temper. The priest was alarmed to find himself holding a fair maid in his arms. He checked the horse, and sprang off it, thinking he faced some new trick of the devil. Young Helga sprang down too, and the child's smock that she wore was so short that it came only to her knee. From the belt of it she snatched her sharp knife, and attacked the startled priest.

"Let me get at you," she screamed. "Let me get at you and plunge my knife in your heart. You are as pale as straw, you beardless slave!"

She closed with him, and fiercely they struggled together, but an unseen power seemed to strengthen the Christian priest. He held her fast, and the old oak tree under which they stood helped him, for it entangled her feet in its projecting roots. With clear water from a nearby spring, the priest sprinkled her neck and face, commanding the unclean spirit to leave her, and blessing her with the sign of the Cross in Christian fashion. But the waters of baptism have no power unless faith wells from within.

Even so, against the evil that struggled within her, he had opposed a power more mighty than his own human strength. Her arms dropped to her sides, as she gazed in pale-faced astonishment at this man whom she took for a mighty magician, skilled in sorcery and in the secret arts. Those were magic runes he had repeated, and mystic signs he had traced in the air. She would not have flinched had he shaken a keen knife or a sharp ax in her face, but she flinched now as he made the sign of the Cross over her head and heart. She sat like a tame bird, with her head drooped upon her breast.

Gently he spoke to her of the great kindness she had shown him during the night, when she had come in the guise of a hideous frog to sever his bonds and to lead him out into light and life again. He said she was bound by stronger bonds than those which had bound him, but that he would lead her out of darkness to eternal life. He would take her to the holy Ansgarius at Hedeby, and there in the Christian city, the spell that had power over her would be broken. But he would not let her sit before him on the horse, even though she wished it. He dared not.

"You must sit behind me on the horse, not in front of me," he said, "for your enchanted beauty has a power that comes of evil, and I fear it. Yet, with the help of the Lord, I shall win through to victory."

He knelt and prayed devoutly and sincerely. It seemed as if the quiet wood became a church, consecrated by his prayers.

The birds began to sing as if they belonged to the new congregation. The wild mint smelled sweet, as if to replace incense and ambergris, and the young priest recited these words from the Bible:

"To give light to them that sit in darkness, and in the shadow of death; to guide our feet into the ways of peace."

While he spoke of the life everlasting, the horse that had carried them in wild career stood quietly by and pulled at the tall bramble bushes until the ripe juicy berries fell into Helga's hand, offering themselves for her refreshment.

Patiently, she let herself be lifted on horseback, and sat there like one in a trance, neither quite awake nor quite asleep. The priest tied two green branches in the shape of a cross, and held it high as they rode through the woods. The shrubs grew thicker and thicker, until at last they rode along in a pathless wilderness.

Bushes of the wild sloe blocked their way so that they had to ride around these thickets. The springs flowed no longer into little streams but into standing ponds, and they had to ride around these, too. But the cool breezes of the forest refreshed and strengthened them, and there was no less strength in the words of faith and Christian love that the young priest found to say, because of his great desire to lead this poor lost soul back to light and life.

They say that raindrops will wear a hollow in the hardest stone, and that the waves of the sea will in time wear the roughest stones smooth and round. Thus did the dew of mercy, which fell on Helga, soften that which was hard, and smooth that which was rough in her nature. Not that any change could yet be seen, or that she knew she was changing, any more than the seed in the ground is aware that the rain and the warm sun will cause it to grow and burst into flower.

When a mother's song unconsciously impresses itself on her child's memory, he babbles the words after her without understanding, but in time, they assume order in his mind and become meaningful to him. Even so, God's healing word began to impress itself on Helga's heart.

They rode out of the wilderness, crossed a heath, and rode on through another pathless forest. There, toward evening, they met with a robber band.

"Where did you kidnap this beautiful wench?" the robbers shouted. They stopped the horse and dragged the two riders from its back.

The priest was surrounded, and he was unarmed except for the knife he had taken from Helga, but with this he now tried to defend her. As one of the robbers swung his ax, the priest sprang aside to avoid the blow, which fell instead on the neck of the horse. Blood spurted forth, and the animal fell to the ground. Startled out of the deep trance in which she had ridden all day, Helga sprang forward and threw herself over the dying horse. The priest stood by to shield and defend her, but one of the robbers raised his iron hammer and brought it down on the priest's head so hard that he bashed it in. Brains and blood spattered about as the priest fell down dead.

The robbers seized little Helga by her white arms, but it was sundown, and as the sun's last beam vanished, she turned back into a frog. The greenish white mouth took up half her face, her arms turned spindly and slimy, and her hands turned into broad, webbed fans. In terror and amazement, the robbers let go of this hideous creature. Froglike she hopped as high as her head and bounded into the thicket. The robbers felt sure this was one of Loki's evil tricks, or some such secret black magic, so they fled from the place in terror.

The full moon rose. It shone in all its splendor as poor frog-shaped Helga crept out of the thicket and crouched beside the slain priest and the slaughtered horse. She stared at them with eyes that seemed to weep, and she gave a sob like the sound of a child about to burst into tears. She threw herself on first one and then the other. She fetched them water in her large hands, which could hold a great deal because of the webbed skin, and poured it over them, but dead they were and dead they would remain. At last, she realized this. Wild animals would come soon and devour their bodies. But no, that must not be!

She dug into the ground as well as she could, trying to make for them a grave as deep as possible. But she had nothing to dig with except the branch of her tree and her own two hands. The webs between her fingers were torn by her labors until they bled, and she made so little headway that she saw the task was beyond her. Then she brought clear water to wash the dead man's face, which she covered with fresh green leaves. She brought large branches to cover him, and scattered dry leaves between them. Then she brought the heaviest stones she could carry, piled them over the body, and filled in the cracks with moss. Now she thought the mound would be strong and safe, but the difficult task had taken her all night long. The sun came up, and there stood young Helga in all her beauty, with blood on her hands and for the first time maidenly tears on her flushed cheeks.

During this transformation, it seemed as if two natures were contending within her. She trembled, and looked about her as if she had just awakened from a nightmare. She took hold of the slender branch of a tree for support. Presently she climbed like a cat to the topmost branches of this tree, and clung there. Like a frightened squirrel, she stayed there the whole day through, in the deep solitude of the forest where all is dead still, as they say.

Dead still! Why, butterflies fluttered all about in play or strife. At the ant hills nearby, hundreds of busy little workmen hurried in and out. The air was filled with countless dancing gnats, swarms of buzzing flies, ladybugs, dragonflies with golden wings, and other winged creatures. Earthworms crawled up from the moist earth, and moles came out. Oh, except for all these, the people might be right when they call the forest "dead still."

No one paid any attention to little Helga except the jays that flew screeching to the tree top where she perched. Bold and curious, they hopped about her in the branches, but there was a look in her eyes that soon put them to flight. They could not make her out, any more than she could understand herself. When evening came on, the setting sun gave warning that it was time for her to change, and it aroused her to activity again. She had no sooner climbed down than the last beam of the sun faded out, and once more she sat there, a shriveled frog with the torn webbed skin covering her hands.

But now her eyes shone with a new beauty that in her lovely form they had not possessed. They were gentle, tender, maidenly eyes. And though they looked out through the mask of a frog, they reflected the deep feelings of a human heart. They brimmed over with tears—precious drops that lightened her heart.

Beside the grave mound lay the Cross of green boughs that had been tied together with bark string, the last work of him who lay buried there. Helga picked it up, and the thought came to her to plant it between the stones that covered the man and the horse. Memory of the priest brought fresh tears to her eyes, and with a full heart she made cross marks in the earth around the grave, as a fence that would guard it well. When with both hands she made the sign of the Cross, the webbed membrane fell from her fingers like a torn glove. She washed her hands at the forest spring, and gazed in amazement at their delicate whiteness. Again, in the air she made the holy sign between herself and the dead man. Her lips trembled, her tongue moved and the name she had heard the priest mention so often during their ride through the woods rose to her lips. She uttered the name of the savior.

The frog's skin fell from her. Once more she was a lovely maiden. But her head hung heavy. She was much in need of rest, and she fell asleep.

However, she did not sleep for long. She awoke at midnight and saw before her the dead horse, prancing and full of life. A shining light came from his eyes and from the wound in his neck. Beside him stood the martyred Christian priest, "more beautiful than Balder," the Viking woman had truly said, for he stood in a flash of flame.

There was such an air of gravity and of righteous justice in the penetrating glance of his great, kind eyes that she felt as if he were looking into every corner of her heart. Little Helga trembled under his gaze, and her memories stirred within her as though this were Judgment Day. Every kindness that had been done her and each loving word spoken to her, were fresh in her mind. Now she understood how it had been love that sustained her through those days of trial, during which all creatures made of dust and spirit, soul and clay, must wrestle and strive. She realized that she had only obeyed the impulse of her inclinations. She had not saved herself. Everything had been given to her, and Providence had guided her. Now, in humility and shame, she bent before him who could read every thought in her heart, and at that moment she felt the pure light of the Holy Spirit enter her soul.

"Daughter of the marsh," the priest said, "out of the earth and the marsh you came, and from this earth you shall rise again. The light in you that is not of the sun but of God, shall return to its source, remembering the body in which it has lain. No soul shall be lost. Things temporal are full of emptiness, but things eternal are the source of life. I come from the land of the dead. Someday, you too shall pass through the deep valley to the shining mountain tops, where compassion and perfection dwell. I cannot lead you to receive Christian baptism at Hedeby, for you must first break the watery veil that covers the deep marsh and bring out of its depths the living source of your birth and your being. You must perform a blessed act before you may be blessed."

He lifted her on the horse and put in her hand a golden censer, like the ones she had seen in the Viking's castle. From it rose a sweet incense, and the wound in the martyr's forehead shone like a diadem. He took the cross from the grave and raised it high as they rose swiftly through the air, over the rustling woods and over the mounds where the heroes of old are buried, each astride his dead war horse. These mighty warriors rose and rode up to the top of the mounds. Golden crowns shone on their foreheads in the moonlight, and their cloaks billowed behind them in the night wind. The dragon on guard over his treasure also lifted his head and watched them pass. Goblins peered up from their hills and hollows, where they swarmed to and fro with red, blue, and green lights as numerous as the sparks of burning paper.

Away over the forest and heath, river and swamp, they hastened until they circled over the Wild Marsh. The priest held aloft the cross, which shone like gold. From his lips fell holy prayers. Little Helga joined in the hymns that he sang, as a child follows its mother's song. She swung the censer, and it gave forth a churchly incense so miraculously fragrant that the reeds and sedges burst into bloom, every seed in the depths sent forth stalks, and all things flourished that had a spark of life within them. Water lilies spread over the surface of the pool like a carpet patterned with flowers, and on this carpet a young and beautiful woman lay asleep. Helga thought this was her own reflection, mirrored in the unruffled water. But what she saw was her mother, the princess from the land of the Nile, who had become the Marsh King's wife.

The martyred priest commanded that the sleeper be lifted up on horseback. Under this new burden, the horse sank down as though his body were an empty, wind-blown shroud. But the sign of the Cross lent strength to the spectral horse, and he carried all three riders back to solid earth.

Then crowed the cock in the Viking's castle, and the spectral figures became a part of the mist that drove before the wind. But the Egyptian princess and her daughter were left there, face to face.

"Is this myself I see, reflected in the deep waters?" cried the mother.

"Is this myself I see, mirrored on the bright surface?" the daughter exclaimed. As they approached one another and met in a heart-to-heart embrace, the mother's heart beat faster, and it was the mother who understood.

"My child! My heart's own flower, my lotus from beneath the waters." She threw her arms about the child and wept. For little Helga, these tears were a fresh baptism of life and love.

"I flew hither in the guise of a swan," Helga's mother told her. "Here I stripped off that plumage and fell into the quagmire. The deep morass closed over me like a wall, and I felt a strong current—a strange power—drag me deeper and deeper. I felt sleep weigh down my eyelids. I slumbered and dreamed. I dreamed that I stood again in the Egyptian pyramid, yet the swaying alder stump that had frightened me so on the surface of the morass stood ever before me. As I watched the check marks in its bark, they took on bright colors and turned into hieroglyphics. I was looking at the casket of a mummy. It burst open, and from it stepped that monarch of a thousand years ago. His mummy was pitch black, a shining, slimy black, like the wood snail or like the mud of the swamp. Whether it was the Marsh King or that mummy of the pyramid, I know not. He threw his arms around me, and I felt that I would die. When I came back to consciousness, I felt something warm over my heart, and there nestled a little bird, twittering and fluttering its wings. From my heart it flew into the heavy darkness overhead, but a long, green strand still bound it to me. I heard and understood its plaintive song, 'To freedom, to the sunlight, to our Father!' Then I remembered my own father, in the sun-flooded land of my birth, my life, and my love. I loosed the strand and let the little bird fly home to my father. From that moment, I have known no other dreams. I have slept, long and deep, until this hour when wondrous sounds and incense woke me and set me free."

What had become of that green strand between the mother's heart and the heart and the bird's wing? Where did it flutter now? What had become of it? Only the stork had ever seen it. That strand was the green stalk, and the bow at the end of it was the bright flower that had cradled the child, who was grown in beauty and now rested once more on her mother's heart.

As they stood there in each other's arms, the stork circled over their heads. Away he flew to his nest for the two sets of swan feathers that he had stored there for so many years. He dropped these sets of feathers upon the mother and daughter, and, once the plumage had covered them, they rose from the ground as two white swans.

"Let's have a chat," said the father stork, "for now we can understand one another, even though different birds have different beaks. It's the luckiest thing in the world that I found you tonight. Tomorrow we shall be on our way, Mother, the young ones, and I, all flying south. Yes, you well may stare. I am your old friend from the banks of the Nile, and Mother is too. Her heart is softer than her beak. She always did say the princess could look out for herself, but I and our sons brought these sets of swan feathers up here. Why, how happy this makes me, and how lucky it is that I am still here. At daybreak we shall set out, with a great company of storks. We shall fly in the vanguard, and if you follow us closely you can't miss your way. The young ones and I will keep an eye on you, too."

"And the lotus flower which I was to fetch," said the Egyptian princess, "now flies beside me in the guise of a swan. I bring with me the flower that touched my heart, and the riddle has been solved. Home we go!"

But Helga said she could not leave the land of the Danes until she had once more seen her good foster mother, the Viking's wife. Helga vividly recalled every fond moment spent with her, every kind word, and even every tear she had caused the foster mother to shed. At that moment she almost felt that she loved her foster mother best of all.

"Yes, we must go to the Viking's castle," said the father stork. "Mother and the young ones are waiting for me there. How their eyes will pop and their beaks will rattle! Mother is no great one for talking. She's a bit curt and dry, but she means very well. Now I must make a great to-do so that they will know we are coming."

So the father stork rattled his beak as he and the swans flew home to the Viking's castle.

Everyone there lay sound asleep. The Viking's wife had gone to bed late that night because she was so worried about Helga, who had been missing ever since the Christian priest disappeared three days ago. She must have helped him escape, for it was her horse that was gone from the stable. But what power could have brought this about? The Viking's wife thought of all the miracles she had heard were performed by the White Christ and by those who had the faith to follow Him. Her troubled thoughts gave way to dreams. She dreamed that she lay there, on her bed, still awake, still lost in thought while darkness reigned outside. A storm blew up. To the east and to the west she heard the high seas roll—waves of the North Sea and waves of the Kattegat. The great snake, which in the depth of the ocean coils around Earth, was in convulsions of terror. It was the twilight of the gods, Ragnarok, as the heathens called Judgment Day, when all would perish, even their highest gods. The war horn sounded, and over the rainbow bridge the gods rode, clad in steel, to fight their last great fight. The winged Valkyries charged on before them, and dead heroes marched behind. The whole firmament blazed with the northern lights, yet darkness conquered in the end. It was an awful hour.

Beside the terror-stricken dreamer, little Helga seemed to crouch on the floor, in the ugly frog's shape. She shuddered, and crept close to her foster mother, who took the creature up in her lap and, hideous though it was, lovingly caressed it. The air resounded with the clashing of swords and clubs, and the rattle of arrows like a hailstorm upon the roof. The hour had come when Heaven and Earth would perish, the stars would fall, and everything be swallowed up by Surtur's sea of fire. Yet she knew there would be a new Heaven and a new Earth. The grain would grow in waving fields where the sea now rolled over the golden sands.

Then the god whose name could not yet be spoken would reign at last, and to him would come Balder, so mild and loving, raised up from the kingdom of the dead. He came, and the Viking's wife saw him clearly. She knew his face, which was that of the captive Christian priest. "The White Christ," she cried aloud, and as she spoke that name she kissed the ugly brow of her frog child. Off fell the frog skin, and it was Helga who stood before her in radiant beauty, gentle as she had never been before, and with beaming eyes. She kissed her foster mother's hands, and blessed her for all the loving kindness that had been lavished upon her in those days of bitter trials and sorrow. She thanked the Viking's wife for the thoughts she had nurtured in her, and for calling upon the name which she repeated—the White Christ. And little Helga arose in the shape of a white, mighty swan. With the rushing sound of a flock of birds of passage taking flight, she spread her powerful wings.

The Viking's wife awakened to hear this very same noise overhead. She knew it was about time for the storks to fly south, and that they must be what she heard. She wanted to see them once more and bid them good luck for their journey, so she got up and went out on her balcony. There, on the roofs of all the outbuildings she saw stork upon stork, and all round the castle bands of storks whirled in widening circles above the high trees. Directly in front of her, beside the well where Helga had so often sat and frightened her with wild behavior, two white swans were sitting. They looked up at her with such expressive eyes that it recalled her dream, which still seemed to her almost real. She thought of Helga in the guise of a swan. She thought of the Christian priest, and suddenly her heart felt glad. The swans waved their wings and bowed their necks to her as if in greeting. The Viking's wife held out her arms as if she understood, and thinking of many things, she smiled at them through her tears.

Then, with a great clattering of beaks and flapping of wings, the storks all started south.

"We won't wait for those swans," said the mother stork. "If they want to go with us they had better come now. We can't dillydally here until the plovers start. It is nicer to travel as we do in a family group, instead of like the finches and partridges, among whom the males and females fly in separate flocks.

I call that downright scandalous. And what kind of strokes do those swans call those that they are making?"

"Oh, everyone has his own way of flying," the father stork said. "Swans fly in a slantwise line, cranes in a triangle, and the plovers in snakelike curves."

"Don't talk about snakes while we are flying up here," said the mother stork. "It will put greedy thoughts in the young ones' heads at a time when they can't be appeased."

"Are those the high mountains of which I have heard?" Helga asked as she flew along in the swan plumage.

"There are thunder clouds, billowing below us," her mother told her.

"And what are the white clouds that rise to such heights?" Helga asked.

"Those heights that you see are the mountains that are always capped with snow," her mother said, as they flew over the Alps, out over the blue Mediterranean.

"African sands! Egyptian strands!" In the upper air through which her swan wings soared, the daughter of the Nile rejoiced when she spied once more the yellow wave-washed coast of her native country. The storks spied it too, and they quickened their flight.

"I can sniff the Nile mud and the juicy frogs," the mother stork cried. "What an appetizing feeling! Yes, there you shall have fine eating and things to see—marabou storks, ibises, and cranes. They are all cousins of ours, but not nearly so handsome as we. They are vain creatures, especially the ibises. The Egyptians stuff them with spices and make mummies of them, and this has quite turned their heads. As for me, I would rather be stuffed with live frogs, and so would you, and so you shall be. Better to have your mouth well stuffed when you are alive than have such a to-do made over you when you are dead. That's the only way I feel about it, and I am always right."

"The storks have come back," said the people in the magnificent home on the banks of the Nile where, on a leopard skin spread over soft cushions in the lofty hall, the master lay between life and death, waiting and hoping for the lotus flower from the deep marshes in the far north. His kinsmen and servants were standing beside his couch, when into the room flew two magnificent white swans who had come with the storks. They doffed their glistening swan feathers, and there stood two lovely women who resembled each other as closely as two drops of water. They bent over the pale, feeble old man, and threw back their long hair. When little Helga leaned above her grandfather, the color returned to his cheeks, light to his eyes, and life to his stiffened limbs. Hale and hearty, the old man rose. His daughter and granddaughter threw their arms around him, as if they were joyously greeting him on the morning after a long and trying dream.

Great was the rejoicing in that house, and in the stork's nest, too, though the storks rejoiced chiefly because of the good food and the abundance of frogs. While the learned men sketchily scribbled down the story of the two princesses, and of the healing flower that had brought such a blessing to that household and throughout all the land, in their own way the parent storks told the story to their children, but not until all of them were full, or they would have had better things to do than listen to stories.

"Now you will become a somebody at last," the mother stork whispered. "It's the least we can expect."

"Oh, what would I become?" said the father stork. "What have I done? Nothing much."

"You have done more than all the others put together. Except for you and our young ones, the two princesses would never have seen Egypt again, nor would the old man have been healed. You will assuredly become a somebody. At the very least, they will give you the title of doctor, and our young ones will inherit it, and their little ones after them. Why, at least to my eyes, you already have the look of an Egyptian doctor."

The wise and learned men propounded the basic principle, as they called it, on which the whole matter rested. "Love brings life," was their doctrine, and this they explained in different ways. "The warm sunbeam was the Egyptian princess. She descended unto the Marsh King, and from their meeting, the flower arose."

"I can't quite repeat the exact words," said the father stork, who had been listening on the roof and wanted to tell his family all about it. "What they said was so incomprehensibly wise that they were given titles and presents too. Even the chief cook was rewarded, no doubt for his soup."

"And what was your reward?" the mother stork wanted to know. "It was not right for them to pass over the most important one in the whole affair, which is just what you are. The learned men did nought but wag their tongues. However, I have no doubt that your turn will come."

Late that night, when the happy household lay peacefully asleep, there was one person left awake. This was not the father stork, who, like a drowsy sentry, stood in his nest on one leg. No, this wide-awake person was little Helga. She leaned over the rail of her balcony and looked up through the clear air at the great shining stars. They were larger and more lustrous than she had ever seen them in the North, but they were the same stars. She thought of the Viking's wife near the Wild Marsh, of her gentle eyes, and of the tears which she had shed over her poor frog child, who now was standing in the splendor of the clear starlight and the wonderful spring air by the waters of the Nile. She thought of the love that filled the heathen woman's heart, the love she had shown that wretched creature who was hateful in her human form and dreadful to see or touch in her animal shape. She looked at the shining stars and was reminded of the glory that had gleamed on the brow of the martyred priest when he flew with her over moor and forest. She recalled the tone of his voice. She recalled those words he had said, when they rode together and she sat like an evil spirit—those words that had to do with that high source of the greatest love that encompasses all mankind throughout all the generations.

Yes, what had she not received, won, gained! Night and day, Helga was absorbed in contemplating her happiness. She regarded it like a child who turns so quickly from the giver to all those wonderful gifts. Her happy thoughts ran on to the even greater happiness that could lie ahead, and would lie ahead. On and on she thought, until she so lost herself in dreams of future bliss that she forgot the giver of all good things. It was the wanton pride of her youth that led her on into the pitfall. Her eyes were bright with pride when a sudden noise in the yard below recalled her straying thoughts. She saw two large ostriches rushing about in narrow circles, and never before had she seen this animal, this huge, fat, and awkward bird. The wings looked as if they had been roughly handled. When she asked why this was, for the first time she heard the legend that Egyptians tell about the ostrich.

Once, they said, the ostriches were a race of glorious and beautiful birds with wings both wide and strong. One evening the other large birds of the forest said to the ostrich, "Brother, shall we fly to the river tomorrow, God willing, and quench our thirst?"

"Yes," the ostrich answered, "so I will." At dawn, away they flew. First they flew aloft toward the sun, which is the eye of God. Higher and higher the ostrich flew, far ahead of all the other birds. In his pride he flew straight toward the light, vaunting his own strength and paying no heed to him from whom strength comes. "God willing," he did not say.

Then, suddenly the avenging angel drew aside the veil from the flaming seas of the sun, and in an instant the wings of that proud bird was burned away, and he wretchedly tumbled to earth. Never since that day has the ostrich or any of his family been able to rise in the air. He can only flee timidly along the ground and run about in circles. He is a warning to us that in all human thoughts and deeds we should say, "God willing."

Helga bowed her head in thoughts. As the ostrich rushed about, she observed how timorous he was and what vain pride he took in the size of the shadow he cast on the white, sunlit wall.

She devoted herself to more serious thoughts. A happy life had been given her, but what was to come of it? Great things, "God willing."

When, in the early spring, the storks made ready to fly north again, Helga took the golden bracelet from her arm and scratched her name upon it. She beckoned to the father stork, slipped the golden band around his neck, and told him to take it to the Viking's wife, as a sign that her adopted daughter was alive, and happy, and had not forgotten her.

"It's a heavy thing to carry," the father stork thought, as he wore it around his neck. "But gold and honor are not to be tossed away on the highroad. The people up there will indeed be saying that the stork brings luck."

"You lay gold and I lay eggs," the mother stork told him, "although you lay only once, while I lay every year. Neither of us gets any thanks for it, which is most discouraging."

"One knows when he's done his duty," the father stork said.

"But you can't hang such knowledge up for all to admire," she said. "Neither will it bring you a favorable wind nor a full meal." Then away they flew.

The little nightingale who sang in the tamarind tree would also be flying north soon. Helga had often heard him singing up near the Wild Marsh. She decided to use him as a messenger, for she had learned the language of the birds when she flew in the guise of a swan, and as she had often talked with the storks and swallows she knew the little nightingale would understand her. She begged him to fly to the beech forest in Jutland, where she had built the tomb of stone and branches. She begged him to tell all the little birds there to guard the grave, and to sing there often. The nightingale flew away—and time went flying by.

That fall, the eagle that perched on the pyramid saw a magnificent caravan of camels, richly laden and accompanied by armed men. These men were splendidly robed and were mounted on prancing Arab horses as white as shining silver, with quivering pink nostrils and big flowing manes that swept down to their slender legs. A royal prince of Arabia, handsome as a prince should be, came as an honored guest to the palace where the storks' nest now stood empty. The nest-owners had been away in the far North, but they would soon return. They did return, on the very evening when the festive celebration was at its height.

It was the wedding that was being celebrated, and the bride was lovely Helga, jeweled and robed in silk. The bridegroom was the young Arabian prince. They sat at the head of the table, between Helga's mother and grandfather. But Helga was not watching the bridegroom's handsome bronzed face, round which his black beard curled. Nor was she looking into the dark, fiery eyes that he fixed upon her. She was staring out at a bright, glistening star that shone down from the sky.

Then there was a rush of wings through the air, and the storks came back. Tired though they were, and badly as they needed rest after their journey, the two old parent storks flew straight to the veranda railing. They knew of the marriage feast, and at the frontier they had already heard news that Helga had commanded their pictures to be painted on the walls, for truly they were a part of her life story.

"That certainly was very nice and thoughtful," said the father stork.

"It was little enough," the mother stork told him. "She could hardly do less."

When Helga saw them, she rose from the table and went out on the veranda to stroke their backs. The old storks bowed their heads, while the youngest of their children looked on and appreciated the honor bestowed on them.

Helga looked up at the bright star, which grew yet more brilliant and clear. Between her and the star hovered a form even purer than the air, and therefore visible through it. As it floated down quite near her, she saw that it was the martyred priest. He too came to her wedding feast—came from the Kingdom of Heaven.

"The splendor and happiness up there," he said, "surpass all that is known on earth."

More humbly and fervently than she had ever yet prayed, Helga asked that for one brief moment she might be allowed to go there and cast a single glance into the bright Kingdom of Heaven. Then he raised her up in splendor and glory, through a stream of melody and thoughts. The sound and the brightness were not only around her but within her soul as well. They lay beyond all words.

"We must go back, or you will be missed," the martyred priest said to her.

"Only one more glance," she begged. "Only one brief moment more."

"We must go back to Earth, for all your guests are leaving."

"Only one more look! The last!"

Then Helga stood again on the veranda, but all the torches had been extinguished, and the banquet hall was dark. The storks were gone. No guests were to be seen, and no bridegroom. All had vanished in those three brief moments.

A great fear fell upon her. She wandered through the huge, empty hall into the next room, where foreign soldiers lay asleep. She opened the side door that led into her own bedroom. When she thought she had entered it, she found herself in the garden, but it wasn't the garden she knew. Red gleamed the sky, for it was the break of day. Only three moments in

Heaven, and a long time had passed on Earth.

She saw the storks and called to them in their own language. The father stork turned his head, listened and came down to her.

"You speak our language," he admitted. "What is your wish, strange woman, and why do you come here?"

"But it is I—Helga. Do you not know me? Only three moments ago we were talking together over there on the veranda."

"You are mistaken," the stork said. "You must have dreamed it."

"No, no!" she said, and reminded him of the Viking's castle, of the Wild Marsh, and of the journey hither.

Then the father stork blinked his eyes. "Why, that is a very old story that my great-great-grandmother told me," he said. "Truly, there once was a princess in Egypt who came from the land of the Danes. But she disappeared on the night of her wedding, hundreds of years ago, and never was seen again. You may read about it yourself, there on the monument in the garden. Swans and storks are carved upon it, and at the top is your own figure, sculptured in white marble."

And this was true. Little Helga saw it, understood it, and dropped upon her knees.

The sun shone brightly in all its splendor. As in the old days when at the first touch of sunlight the frog's skin fell away to reveal a beautiful maiden, so now, in that baptism by the sun a form of heavenly beauty, clearer and purer than the air itself, rose as a bright beam to join the Father. The body crumbled to dust, and only a wilted lotus flower lay where she had knelt.

"Well," said the father stork. "That's a new ending to the

story. I hadn't expected it, but I liked it quite well."

"How will the young ones like it?" the mother stork wondered.

"Ah," said the father stork, "that certainly is the most important thing, after all."

THE STONE OF THE WISE MAN (1858)

You know the story of Holger Danske, so we won't repeat it, but will ask you if you remember how "Holger Danske conquered the great land of India, eastward at the end of the world, to the tree called 'the Tree of the Sun,'" as Christen Pedersen says. Do you know Christen Pedersen? It makes no difference if you don't.

Holger Danske gave Prester John his power and rule over India. Have you heard about Prester John? Yes? Well, it makes no difference if you haven't, because he doesn't come into our story. You are going to hear about the Tree of the Sun "in India, eastward at the end of the world," as people believed it to be then, for they hadn't studied their geography the way we have—but that makes no difference, either!

The Tree of the Sun was a magnificent tree, such as we have never seen and most likely never will see. Its crown stretched out for miles around; it was really an entire wood, for each of its smallest branches formed, in turn, a whole tree. Palms, beech pines, plane trees, yes, and many other kinds of trees grew here, trees that are to be found all over the world; they sprang forth, as small branches, from the great branches, and these, with their knots and windings, were like hills and valleys, carpeted with soft, velvety green and covered with thousands of flowers. Each branch was like a great blooming meadow or the most beautiful garden. The blessed Sun shone down upon it, for, remember, it was the Tree of the Sun.

Here the birds from all over the world gathered together, birds from the primeval forests of America, the rose gardens of Damascus, or the wild woods of Africa, where the elephant and the lion imagine that they alone reign. Polar birds came here, and the stork and swallow naturally did, too. But the birds were not the only living creatures here; the stag, the squirrel, the antelope, and hundreds of other beautiful and light-footed animals were at home in this place. The crown of the tree was a spreading, fragrant garden, and in the very center of it, where the great branches rose up into a green hill, there stood a castle of crystal, with a view toward every country in the world. Each tower rose up in the form of a lily, and one could ascend through the stem, for inside there were winding stairs. One could step out onto the leaves—these were the balconies; and up in the cup of the flower was a beautiful, brilliant round hall, with no roof above it, only the blue sky, with either the sun or the stars.

Down below, in the wide halls of the castle, there was just as much splendor, though of a different sort. Here the whole world was reflected on the walls. One could see everything that happened, so there was no need to read newspapers; there were no newspapers here, anyway. Everything could be seen in living pictures, if one wanted to or was able to see it all; for too much is too much, even for the wisest man. And the wisest of all men lived here.

His name is too difficult for you to pronounce, and it makes no difference, anyway. He knew everything that a man on Earth can know or hope to know; he knew every invention that had been made or was yet to be made; but he knew nothing more than that, for everything in the world has its limits. Wise old

King Solomon was only half as wise as this man, and yet he was very wise indeed, and governed the forces of nature and ruled over mighty spirits; even Death itself was forced to report every morning with a list of those who were to die during the day. But King Solomon himself had to die, too, and this was the thought that often occupied the mind of the learned, mighty ruler of the castle on the Tree of the Sun. However high he might rise above men in wisdom, he also must die someday. He knew that he and his children, too, must fade like the leaves of the forest and become dust. He could see the human race fade away like leaves on the trees and new men come forth to take their places. But the leaves that fell never lived again; they became dust about other plants.

What happened to man when the Angel of Death came to him? What could Death be? The body became decayed. And the soul? Yes, what was the soul? What became of it? Where did it go? "To the life eternal," the comforting voice of religion said. But what was the transition? Where did one dwell, and how? "In Heaven above," said the pious people, "it is there we go." "Above?" repeated the Wise Man, and gazed up at the Moon and stars. "Up there?"

From the earthly globe, he saw that "above" and "below" could be one and the same, depending upon where one stood on the revolving earth. And if he ascended as high as Earth's loftiest mountains rear their peaks, there in the air that we below call clear and transparent—"the pure heaven"—would be a black darkness, spread over all like a cloth, and the sun would have a coppery glow without giving forth rays, and our Earth would lie wrapped in an orange mist. How narrow were the limits of the mortal eye, and how little could be seen by the eye of the soul! Even the wisest knew little of that which is the most important of all to us.

In the most secret chamber of that castle lay Earth's greatest treasure—the Book of Truth. Page after page, the Wise Man had read it through. Every man may read in this book, but only parts of it; to many an eye the letters seem to fade, so that the words cannot even be spelled; on some pages, the writing is so pale that they seem like blank leaves. But the wiser a man becomes, the more he can read; and the wisest men read the most. The Wise Man knew how to unite the sunlight and the starlight with the light of reason and the hidden powers of his soul, and under this dazzling light, many things stood out clearly on the pages before him. But in the chapter of the book entitled "Life After Death" there was not so much as one single letter to see. That grieved him. Could he not somewhere on Earth obtain a light by which everything written in the Book of Truth would become clear to him?

Like wise King Solomon, he understood the language of the animals and could interpret their talk and their songs. But that made him none the wiser. He had learned the powers of plants and metals, powers that could be used for the cure of diseases or for delaying death, but none that could destroy death. In all created things that he could reach, he sought the light that would shine upon the certainty of eternal life, but he did not find it. Blank leaves still appeared in the Book of Truth before him. Christianity gave him words of promise of an eternal life in the Bible, but he wanted to read it in his book; and there he could see nothing about it.

The Wise Man had five children, four sons, educated as well as the sons of the wisest of fathers should be, and a daughter, lovely, gentle, and clever, but blind. Yet this affliction was no deprivation to her, for her father and brothers were mortal eyes to her, and her own keen perception gave her clear mental vision.

The sons had never ventured farther from the castle than the extent of the branches of the tree, nor had the sister ever left the home. They were happy children in the home of their childhood—the beautiful, fragrant Tree of the Sun. Like all children, they were happy to have stories told them, and their father told them many things that other children would never have understood, but these children were as clever as most of our old people are. He explained to them the pictures of life that they saw on the castle walls—the labors of men and the march of events in all the lands of Earth. Often the sons wished that they could go into the world and take part in the great deeds of other men, and then their father explained to them that it was hard and wearisome out in the world, that the world was not as they saw it from their beautiful home.

He told them of the good, the true, and the beautiful, and explained that these three clung together in the world, and that under the pressure they endured they hardened into a precious stone, purer than the water of a diamond—a splendid jewel of value to God Himself, whose brightness outshone all things; this was called the "Stone of the Wise Man." He told them that, just as man could gain knowledge of the existence of God by seeking it, so was it within the power of man to gain proof that such a jewel as the Stone of the Wise Man existed. This explanation would have been beyond the understanding of other children, but these children could grasp it, and in time other children, too, will learn to understand its meaning.

They asked their father about the true, the beautiful, and the good, and he told them many things—how when God made man from the dust of the earth, he gave to his work five kisses—fiery kisses, heart kisses—which we now call the five senses. Through these, that which is the true, the beautiful, and the good is seen, felt, and understood; through them, it is valued, protected, and augmented. Five senses have been given, physically and mentally, inwardly and outwardly, to body and soul.

By day and by night, the children thought deeply about all these things. Then the eldest of the brothers had a wonderful dream; and, strangely enough, the second brother had the same dream, and the third did, too, and the fourth—all of them dreamed exactly the same thing. They dreamed that each went out into the world and found the "Stone of the Wise Man," which gleamed like a radiant light on his forehead when, in the morning dawn, he rode his swift horse back over the velvety green meadows of home to the castle of his father. Then the jewel threw such a divine light and brilliance upon the pages of the book that everything written there on the life beyond the grave was illuminated. But the sister dreamed nothing about venturing out into the world, for it had never entered her mind. Her world was her father's castle.

"I shall ride out into the wide world," said the eldest brother. "I must find what life is like there, and mix with people. I shall do only what is good and true, and with these I shall protect the beautiful. Many things shall change for the better when I am there."

Yes, his thoughts were bold and big, as our thoughts always are at home, before we have gone out into the world and have met with wind and rain, thorns and thistles.

Now in all of these brothers the five senses were highly developed, both inwardly and outwardly; but in each of them one sense had reached a keenness surpassing the other four. In the case of the eldest, this outstanding sense was sight. This was to be of special benefit to him. He had eyes for all times, he said, and eyes for all nations, eyes that could look into the very depths of the earth, where treasures lie hidden, or into the depths of people's hearts, as though only a clear pane of glass were before them; in other words, he saw more than we could in the cheek that blushes or turns pale, in the eye that cries or laughs.

Stags and antelopes escorted him to the western boundaries of his home, and there the wild swans received him and led him on into the northwest. And now he was far out into the world, far from the land of his father, which extended eastward to the ends of Earth.

How widely his eyes opened in amazement! There were many things to be seen here; and things appear very different when a man look at them with his own eyes instead of merely at a picture, as he had done in his father's house, however good the picture may be, and those in his father's house were unusually good. At first he nearly lost his eyes in astonishment at all the rubbish, all the carnival-like decorations that were supposed to represent the beautiful; but he did not quite lose them, and soon found full use for them. He wished to work thoroughly and honestly to understand the beautiful, the true, and the good. But how were these represented in the world? He saw that often the praise which by right belonged to the beautiful was given to the ugly; that the good was often overlooked, and mediocrity was applauded when it should have been hissed. People looked at the dress and not at the wearer, asked for a name instead of a value, and were guided more by reputation than by worth. It was the same everywhere.

"I must attack these things," he thought, and he did so.

But while he was seeking the truth there came the Devil, who is the father of all lies. Gladly would he have plucked out the eyes of this seer, but that would have been too blunt, for the Devil works in a more cunning way. He let him continue to seek and see the true and the good; but while the young man was doing so, the Devil blew a mote into his eye, into both eyes, one mote after another; this, of course, would harm even the clearest sight. Then the fiend blew upon the motes until they became beams, and the eyes were destroyed. There the Seer stood like a blind man in the great world and had no faith in it, for he had lost his good opinion of it and of himself. And when a man loses confidence in the world and himself, it is all over with him.

"All over!" sang the wild swans, flying across the sea toward the east. "All over!" repeated the swallows, also flying eastward toward the Tree of the Sun. It was not good news that they were carrying to the young man's home.

"The Seer must have done badly," said the second brother, "but the Hearer may have better luck." For in this son the sense of hearing was developed to a very high degree; so keen was it that he could hear the very grass grow.

He lovingly bade farewell and rode away from home, full of sound abilities and good intentions. The swallows followed him, and he followed the swans, until he was far from his home, far out in the wide world.

Then he discovered that one may have too much of a good things. For his hearing was too fine. Not only could he hear the grass grow, but he could hear every man's heart beat, whether in sorrow or in joy. To him the whole world was like the great workshop of a clockmaker, with all the clocks going "Tick, tock," and all the tower clocks striking "Ding, dong." The noise was unbearable. For a long time his ears held out, but at last all the noise, the shrieking, became too much for one man. Then "street boys" of some sixty years of age—for years alone don't make men—raised a tumult, at which the Hearer would have laughed, except for the slanderous talk that followed and echoed through every house and street; it was heard even in the country lanes. Falsehood pushed itself forward and pretended to be the master; bells on the fools' caps jangled and insisted they were church bells, until the noise became too much for the Hearer and he thrust his fingers into his ears. But still he could hear false singing and evil sounds, gossip and idle words, scandal and slander, groaning and moaning, on all sides—none of it worth listening to. Heaven help us! It was impossible to endure; it was all too mad! He thrust his fingers deeper and deeper into his ears, until at last his eardrums burst. Now he heard nothing at all; he could not hear the true, the beautiful, and the good; his hearing was to have been the bridge by which he would have crossed to it. He became morose and suspicious, at last trusting no one, not even himself, and that was most unfortunate. He would not be able to discover and bring home the divine jewel, and so he gave up; he even gave himself up, and that was the worst of all. The birds that flew eastward brought the tidings of this also to the father's castle in the Tree of the Sun; no letters arrived there, for there was no mail service.

"Now I'll try," said the third brother. "I have a sharp nose."

It wasn't a very good practice for him to boast like that, but that was his way, and we must take him as he was. He had a happy disposition and was a poet, a great poet; he could sing many things that he could not speak, and ideas came to him far more quickly than they did to others.

"I can smell a rat!" he said. And it was his highly developed sense of smell to which he attributed his great range of knowledge about the realm of the beautiful.

"Every fragrant spot in the realm of the beautiful has its denizens," he said. "Some like the smell of apple blossoms; some like the smell of a stable. One man is at home in the atmosphere of the tavern, among the smoking tallow candles, where the smell of spirits mingles with the fumes of cheap tobacco. Another prefers to be near the heavy scent of jasmine, or to scent himself with strong oil of cloves. Some seek the fresh sea breezes, while others climb the highest mountain to look down on the bustling little life beneath."

Yes, thus he spoke. It seemed to him as if he had already been out in the wide world and known people from close association with them. But this conviction arose from within himself; it was the poet within him, the gift Heaven had bestowed on him in his cradle.

He bade farewell to his ancestral home in the Tree of the Sun and went on foot through the pleasant countryside. When he arrived at the boundaries of his home, he mounted an ostrich, which runs faster than a horse, and when he later met the wild swans, he swung himself onto the strongest of them, for he loved variety. Away he flew across the sea to distant lands of great forests, deep lakes, towering mountains, and proud cities. And wherever he appeared it seemed as if sunlight traveled with him across the countryside, for every flower and bush gave forth a new fragrance, conscious that nearby was a friend and protector who understood them and knew their value. Then the crippled rosebush stretched out its branches, opened its leaves, and gave bloom to the most beautiful roses; even the black, slimy wood snail saw its beauty.

"I will put my mark on the flower," said the snail. "Now I have spit on it, and there is nothing more I can do for it."

"Thus the beautiful always fares in this world!" said the Poet.

Then he sang a song about it in his own way, but nobody listened. So he gave a drummer two pennies and peacock's feather, and then arranged the song for the drum, and had it drummed throughout the town, in all the streets and lanes. When the people heard it they said that they understood it—it was very profound!

And so the Poet sang other songs about the beautiful, the good, and the true, and people listened to them among the smoking tavern candles, listened in the fresh meadows, in the forests, and on the high seas. It seemed as if this brother was going to have better luck than the other two.

But that angered the Devil, and so he promptly set to work with all the incense powder and smoke to be found, the very strongest, which can stifle anyone, and which he can prepare artfully enough to even confuse an angel—and surely, therefore, a poor poet! The Devil knows how to take hold of a man like that! He surrounded the Poet so completely with incense that the poor man lost his head, forgot his mission, his home, everything—even himself; he then vanished in smoke.

When the little birds heard about this they were sad, and for three days they didn't sing. The black wood snail became blacker still, not from grief but from envy.

"They should have burned incense for me," he said, "for it was I who gave him the idea for the most famous of his songs, the drum song about the way of the world. It was I who spat at the rose! I can bring witnesses to prove that!"

But no news of this reached the Poet's home in India, for all the little birds were mourning and silent for three days; and when their time of mourning was over, their grief had been so profound that they had forgotten for whom they wept. That's the way it goes.

"Now I'll have to go into the world and stay away like the others," said the fourth brother.

He had as good a humor as the third, though he was no poet, which was a fine reason for him to have a good humor. Those two had filled the castle with gaiety, and now the last of that gaiety was leaving. Men have always considered sight and hearing the two most important senses, those that it is most desirable to strengthen and sharpen; the other three senses are generally looked upon as subordinate. But that was not the belief of this son, for he had especially cultivated his taste in every way possible, and taste is very powerful indeed. It governs what goes into the mouth and into the mind; hence this brother tasted everything there was in pots and pans, in bottles and barrels, explaining that this was the uncouth side of his function. To him every man was a vessel with something cooking within, and every country was an enormous kitchen, a kitchen of the mind—this he considered fine indeed, and he wanted to go out into the world and taste of it.

"Perhaps I'll have better luck than my brothers. I shall be on my way—but how shall I travel? Are balloons invented yet?" he asked his father, who knew about all inventions that had been made or would be in the future. But men had not yet invented balloons, or steamships, or railways. "Then I'll go by balloon," he said. "My father knows how they're made and steered, and that I can learn. They aren't invented yet, so people will think it's some spirit of the air. When I have finished with the balloon I'll burn it, and for that you must give me some pieces of another invention to come—matches."

When he had received what he wanted, he flew away. The birds flew much farther along with him than they had with his brothers. They were curious to know how the flight would come out, for they thought it was some new kind of bird. More and more came sweeping up until the air was black with birds; they came on like the cloud of locusts over the land of Egypt. And so now he, the last brother, was out in the wide world.

"The East Wind is a good friend and helper to me," he said.

"You mean the East Wind and the West Wind!" said the winds. "You couldn't have flown northwest if we both hadn't helped you."

But he didn't hear what the wind said, and that makes no difference. The birds tired of flying along with the balloon. Too much had been made of that thing, said a pair of them. It had become conceited! "It isn't worth flying with; it's nothing!" And then they withdrew; they all withdrew, for indeed too much had been made of nothing.

The balloon descended over one of the greatest cities, and the aeronaut landed on the highest point, the church steeple.

The balloon rose into the air again, which it shouldn't have done; we don't know where it went, but that doesn't matter, for it was not yet invented. There the young man sat on the church steeple, the birds no longer hovering around him; he had grown as tired of them as they had of him.

All the chimneys of the town smoked fragrantly.

"Those are altars erected in your honor," said the Wind, which thought it ought to say something pleasant.

He sat up there boldly and gazed down at the people in the streets. One person was prancing along, proud of his purse; another was proud of the key that hung at his girdle, though he had nothing for it to unlock; one was proud of his moth-eaten coat, another of his worm-eaten body.

"Vanity!" he said. "I must go down, dip my fingers into that pot, and taste it. But I'll sit here a little longer, for the wind is blowing very pleasantly against my back; I'll take a little rest. 'It is good to sleep long in the mornings, when one has much to do,' the lazy man says. Laziness is the root of all evil, but there is no evil in our family. I'll stay here as long as the wind blows, for it feels good."

So he sat there; but since he was sitting on the weathercock of the steeple, which turned round and round with him, he had the false idea that the same wind was still blowing, so he remained seated there; he might as well stay a long while and have a good taste.

Back in India, in the castle of the Tree of the Sun, it had become empty and quiet after the brothers, one after another, had gone away.

"Things are going badly with them," said the father. "Never will they bring home the gleaming jewel; it is not for me. They are all dead and gone!" And then he bent over the Book of Truth and gazed at the page that should have told him of life after death, but there was nothing for him to see or learn from it.

Now his blind daughter was his sole joy and consolation; she clung to him with deep affection, and for the sake of his happiness and peace of mind she wished the precious jewel might be discovered and brought home. With sorrow and longing she thought of her brothers. Where were they? Where could they be living? With all her heart she wished she might dream of them, but strangely enough, not even in her dreams could she reach them.

At last one night she dreamed that their voices sounded across to her, calling to her from out in the wide world, and she could not hold back, but traveled far, far away; and yet she seemed still to be in her father's house. She never met her brothers, but in her dream she felt a sort of fire burning in her hand that did not pain her—it was the shining jewel she was bringing to her father.

When she awoke she thought for a moment that she still held the stone in her hand, but it was the knob of her distaff that she was grasping. Through that long night she had spun incessantly, and on the distaff was a thread finer than the finest spider's web; human eyes could not distinguish the separate threads in it, so fine were they. She had moistened it with her tears, and it was as strong as a rope. She arose; her decision was made—the dream must become a reality.

It was still night, and her father was sleeping. She pressed a kiss on his hand, and then, taking her distaff, fastened the end of the thread to her father's castle. But for this, in her blindness she would never have been able to find her way home; she must hold fast to that thread and trust neither to herself nor to others. From the Tree of the Sun she broke off four leaves; these she would entrust to the winds to bring to her brothers as letters of greeting in case she should not meet them out there in the wide world.

How could she fare, that poor blind child? She could hold fast to her invisible thread. She possessed one gift that all the others lacked—sensibility—and by virtue of this she seemed to have eyes in the very tips of her fingers and ears in her heart.

Then she went forth quietly into the noisy, whirling, strange world, and wherever she went the sky became so bright with sunshine that she could feel the warm rays; and the rainbow spread itself through the blue air where there had been dark clouds. She heard the birds sing, and smelled the scent of orange groves and apple orchards so strongly that she seemed to taste the fruit. Soft tones and delightful sounds reached her ears, but with them came howlings and roarings; manifold thoughts and opinions strangely contradicted each other. The echoes of human thoughts and feelings penetrated into the depths of her heart. One chorus sounded mournfully,

Our earthly life is filled with mist and rain;
And in the dark of night we cry with pain!
But then she heard a brighter strain,
Our earthly life is like a rosebush, so bright;
It is filled with sunshine and true delight!
And if one chorus sounded bitterly,
Each person thinks of himself alone;
This truth to us is often shown.

from the other side came the answer,
Throughout our life a Fairy of Love
Guides our steps from Heaven above.
She could hear the words,
There's pettiness here, far and wide;
Everything has its wrong side.
But then she heard,
So much good is done here
That never reaches man's ear.
And if sometimes the mocking words sounded to her,
Make fun of everything, laugh in jest,
Laugh along with all the rest!
a stronger voice came from the Blind Girl's heart,
Trust in God and thyself; pray then
His will be done forever; amen.

Whenever the Blind Girl entered the circle of humanity and appeared among people, young or old, knowledge of the true, the good, and the beautiful was radiant in their hearts. Wherever she went, whether she entered the studio of the artist, or the hall decorated for the feast, or the crowded factory with its whirring wheels, it seemed as though a sunbeam were entering, as though the string of a lute sounded, or a flower exhaled its perfume, or a refreshing dewdrop fell upon a withering leaf.

But the Devil could not put up with this. With more cunning than that of ten thousand men, he devised a way to bring about his purpose. From the marsh he collected little bubbles of stagnant water and muttered over them a sevenfold echo of untrue words, to give them strength. Then he blended bought heroic poems and lying epitaphs, as many as he could find, boiled them in the tears of envy, colored them with grease paint he had scraped from the faded cheeks of an old lady, and from all this he fashioned a maiden with the appearance and carriage of the Blind Girl, the blessed angel of sensibility. Then the Devil's plot was consummated, for the world knew not which of the two was the true one, and indeed how could the world know?

Trust in God and thyself; pray then
His will be done, forever; amen.

sang the Blind Girl in complete faith. Then she entrusted to the winds the four green leaves from the Tree of the Sun as letters of greeting to her brothers, and she was quite sure that they would reach their destinations and the jewel be found, the jewel that dims all the glories of the world. From the forehead of humanity it would gleam even to the house of her father.

"Even to the house of my father," she repeated. "Yes, the place of the jewel is on this earth, and I shall bring with me more than the promise of it. I can feel its glow; in my closed hand it swells larger and larger. Every grain of truth, however fine it was, which the wind whirled toward me, I caught up and treasured; I let penetrate into it the fragrance of the beautiful, of which there is so much in the world, even for the blind. To the first I added the sound of the beating heart, doing good. I bring only dust with me, but still it is the dust of the jewel we sought, and it is in ample quantity. I have my whole hand full of it!"

Then she stretched forth her hand toward her father. She was home. She had traveled there with the swiftness of thoughts in flight, having never let go of the invisible thread leading to home.

With the fury of a hurricane, the evil powers swept over the

Tree of the Sun, and their wind blasts rushed through the open doorway, into the sanctuary of the Book of Truth.

"It will be blown away by the wind!" cried the father, and he seized the hand she had opened.

"Never!" she replied with calm assurance. "It cannot be blown away; I can feel the rays warming my very soul."

And the father became aware of a dazzling flame, right where the shining dust poured from her hand onto the Book of Truth, that would grant the certainty of an everlasting life. Now on the white page there glowed one shining word—one word only—

BELIEVE

And once more the four brothers were with their father and sister. When the green leaf had fallen upon the bosom of each, a great longing for home had taken hold of them and led them back; the birds of passage had followed them, as had the stag, the antelope, and all the wild creatures of the forest, for all wished to share in their joys—and why shouldn't they when they could?

We have often seen how a column of dust whirls around where a sunbeam bursts through a crack in a door into a dusty room. But this was not common, insignificant dust; even the colors of the rainbow are lifeless compared with the beauty that showed itself here. From the page of the book, from the glowing word Believe, arose each grain of truth, decked with the loveliness of the beautiful and the good, flaming more brightly than the mighty pillar of fire that led Moses and the children of Israel to the land of Canaan. And from the word Believe arose the bridge of Hope, extending to the eternal love in the realm of the Infinite.

THE A-B-C BOOK (1858)

Once there was a man who had written some new rhymes for the A-B-C Book—two lines for each letter, just as in the old A-B-C Book. He believed the old rhymes were too antiquated, that something new was needed, and he thought well indeed of his own rhymes.

His new A-B-C Book was still only in handwriting, and already it had been placed beside the old printed one in the great bookcase where there stood many books, both of knowledge and for amusement. But the old A-B-C Book didn't want to be a neighbor to the new one, and therefore had sprung down from the shelf and at the same time had given the new one a push, so that it, as well as the old one, now lay on the floor, with all its loose leaves scattered about.

The old A-B-C Book lay open at the first page—and that is the most important page, for there all the letters, large and small, are displayed. That one page contains on it the essence of all the books that ever were written; it contains the alphabet, that wonderful army of signs which rules the world; truly a marvelous power they have! Everything depends on the order in which they are commanded to stand; they have the power to give life or to kill, to gladden and to sadden. Separately they mean nothing, but marshaled and ranked in word formations, what can they not accomplish! Yes, when God put them into man's thoughts, human strength became inferior to that which lay in the alphabet, and we yielded with a deep bow.

There, then, they lay now, facing upward, and the Cock which was pictured at the big A of the alphabet gleamed with feathers of red, blue, and green. Proudly he puffed himself up and ruffled his plumage, for he knew how important the letters were and that he was the only living thing among them.

When he found the old A-B-C Book had fallen open on the floor, he flapped his wings, flew out, and perched himself on a corner of the bookcase. There he preened himself with his beak and crowed loudly and long. Every single book in the case, all of which would stand day and night, as if in a trance when nobody was reading them, was roused by his trumpet call. Then the Cock spoke out loudly and clearly about the way the worthy old A-B-C Book had been insulted.

"Everything has to be new and different nowadays," he said. "Everything has to be advanced. Children are so wise that they can read before they have even learned the alphabet. 'They should have something new!' said the man who wrote those new verses sprawling there on the floor. I know them all by heart; he admires them so much that I have heard him read them aloud more than ten times over. No, I prefer my own, the good old rhymes with Xanthus for X, and with the pictures that belong to them! I'll fight for them and crow for them! Every book in the case here knows them very well. Now I'll read aloud these new rhymes. I'll try to read them patiently, and I know we'll all agree they're worthless.

A—Adam

Had Adam obeyed, he'd not have had to leave
The Garden where first dwelt he and Eve.

B—Bank; Bee

The Bank is a place where you put your money;

The Bee is an insect that gathers honey.

"Now that verse I find profoundly insipid!" said the Cock. "But I'll read on.

C—Columbus

Columbus sailed the ocean to the distant shore,

And then the Earth became twice as big as before.

D—Denmark

About the kingdom of Denmark, there's a saying which goes

God's hand protects it, as every Dane knows.

"That many people will consider beautiful," said the Cock. "But I don't. I see nothing beautiful about it. But I'll go on.

E—Elephant

The Elephant has a heavy step,

Though young in heart and full of pep.

F—Face

The Moon above feels at its best

When an eclipse gives its Face a rest.

G—Goat

It is easier to sail a boat

Than to teach manners to a Goat!

H—Hurrah

Hurrah is a word we often hear;

How often does the deed merit such cheer?

"How will a child understand that!" said the Cock. "I suppose they'll put on the title page, 'A-B-C Book for Big People and Little People'; but the big people have something else to do besides read the rhymes in A-B-C Books, and the little people won't be able to understand them. There is a limit to everything. But to continue:

J—Job

We have a Job to do on Earth
Till Earth becomes our final berth.
"Now, that's crude!" said the Cock.
K—Kitten
When Kittens grow up we call them cats
And hope they'll catch our mice and rats.
L—Lion
The savage Lion has much more sense
Than the arty critic's stinging offense!
"How are you going to explain that one to children?" said the Cock.
M—Morning Sun
The golden Morning sun arose,
But not because of the cock's crows.
"Now he's getting personal!" said the Cock. "But then I'm in excellent company. I'm in company with the sun. Let's go on.
N—Negro
Black is a Negro, black as Night,
And we cannot wash him white!
O—Olive Leaf
The best of leaves—you know its name?
The dove's Olive leaf—of Bible fame.
P—Peace
That Peace may ever reign, far and near,
Is indeed a hope we all hold dear.
Q—Queen; Quack
A Queen is a lady of royal position.
A Quack is a fake and not a physician.
R—Round
One may be Round and well extended,

But that doesn't mean one is well descended!

S—Swine

Be not a braggart; be honest and true,

Though many Swine in the forest belong to you!

"Will you permit me to crow!" said the Cock. "It tries your strength, reading so much; I must catch my breath." And then he crowed, shrill as a trumpet of brass, and it was a great pleasure to listen to—for the Cock. "I'll go on.

T—Teakettle; Tea Urn

The Teakettle in the kitchen will always belong,

And yet to the Tea urn it gives its song.

U—Universe

Our Universe will always be,

Through ages to eternity.

"Now that is meant to be deep!" said the Cock. "It's so deep I can't get to the bottom of it!

W—Washerwoman

A Washerwoman will wash and scrub

Until there's nothing left but the tub!

"Now, it's certainly impossible that he can have found anything new for X.

X—Xantippe

In the sea of marriage are rocks of strife,

As Socrates found with Xantippe, his wife.

"He would have to take Xantippe! Xanthus is much better.

Y—Ygdrasil

Under Ygdrasil tree the gods sat every day;

But the tree is dead and the gods have gone away.

"Now we are almost through," said the Cock. "That's a relief. I'll continue on.

Z—Zephyr

Zephyr, in Danish, is a west wind so cold
It penetrates fur and skin, we're told.

"That's that. But that's not the end of it. Now it will be printed and then it will be read. It will be offered in place of the noble old rhymes in my book. What says this assembly—learned and not so learned, single volumes and collected works? What says the alphabet? I have spoken; now let the others act."

The books stood still, and the bookcase stood still; but the Cock flew back to his place at the capital A in the old A-B-C Book and looked proudly around. "I have spoken well, and I have crowed well. The new A-B-C Book can't do anything like that. It will certainly die; in fact, it's dead already, for it has no Cock!"

THE WIND TELLS ABOUT VALDEMAR DAAE AND HIS DAUGHTERS (1859)

When the wind sweeps over the grass, the blades of grass ripple like the water of a lake; and when it sweeps over the cornfield, the ears of corn curl into waves like those on a lake; this is the dance of the Wind. But listen to him tell the story; he sings it out; and how different his song among the trees of the forest is from his shriek through the cracks, crannies, and crevices of old walls. Watch him chase the white, fleecy clouds across the sky like a flock of sheep; notice how he howls through the open gate, as if he were the watchman blowing his horn. Strangely he whistles through the chimney until the fire on the hearth beneath blazes up, and it is pleasant and comfortable to sit in the chamber warmed by its glow and listen to stories. Let only the Wind himself be the storyteller! He knows more wonderful tales than all the rest of us put together. Hear now how he tells the story: "Whew, whew, whew! On, on, on!" That is the theme of his song.

"Near the Great Belt there stands an old mansion with thick red walls," says the Wind. "I know every stone of those walls; I knew them in the olden days when they were part of Marsk Stig's castle on the promontory. They were torn down from there, but then they were built up again to form a new wall and a new mansion; this was Borreby Mansion, which stands to this day. I have seen and known all the noble men and women of many different families who have lived there. Now I shall tell you of Valdemar Daae and his daughters.

"He was a very proud man, for he was of royal blood. He knew more than how to hunt the stag or empty the jug. 'Everything will come out right,' he used to say.

"His highborn wife walked daintily in her golden-cloth garment over floors of polished mosaic. Magnificent tapestries and costly, beautifully carved furniture surrounded her; she had brought both silver and gold into the house; there was German beer in the cellar; proud black horses neighed in the stables; ah, Borreby Mansion was then the home of wealth. And there were children; three fair daughters—I can still remember their names—Ide, Johanne, and Anna Dorothea. These were rich folk, noble folk, born and reared in luxury. Whew, whew, whew! On, on, on!" sang the Wind, and then continued his tale.

"Here I never saw, as in other old houses, the noble mistress turning the spinning wheel among her maidens in the great hall. She played upon the lute and sang, though not always the old Danish songs, but songs in foreign languages. There were life and gaiety here; guests of distinction came from far and near; the sounds of music and the clinking of glasses were so loud that even I could not drown them. There was pride here, with boasting and bragging, and talk of domination, but not the blessings of our Lord!

"Then there was one May Day even," said the Wind, "when I came upon it from the west. I had seen ships wrecked on the coast of West Jutland, had hunted over the heath and the green-wooded shore to Fünen, and now I came over the Great Belt, blowing and roaring. I lay down for a rest on the coast of Zeeland, quite near Borreby Mansion, where the beautiful forest of oaks still grew. The young lads of the neighborhood came out to the forest to collect the biggest and driest branches and twigs they could find; they carried them into the town, laid them in piles, set fire to them, then the young men and girls sang as they danced around them.

"I lay still," said the Wind, "but then gently I just touched one of the branches that had been brought by the handsomest lad of them all, and immediately his pile of wood blazed up the highest. That meant he became the leader among them, with the privilege of choosing first one of the young girls to be his own May lamb. There was a joy, a merriment, such as I had never found in the rich Borreby Mansion.

"Then there came driving toward the mansion, in a gilded carriage drawn by six horses, the noble lady herself with her three daughters—so young and so fair—three sweet blossoms, a rose, a lily, and a pale hyacinth. Their mother was like a proud, splendid tulip; no word of greeting did she have for the peasants, who stopped their game and bowed and scraped to her; stiff as a tulip she held herself. Yes, rose, lily, and pale hyacinth, I saw all three; whose May lambs would they become one day, I wondered. Surely their young men would be proud knights, perhaps even princes! Whew, whew, whew! On, on, on!

"So the carriage rattled past, and the peasants returned to their dance. Summer was being celebrated from one town to another, in Borreby, Tjaereby, and all the towns around.

"But when I rose up that same night, the highborn lady had laid herself down, never to rise again. That had come to her which comes to all men; that is nothing new. Grave and thoughtful stood Valdemar Daae; he seemed to be saying, 'The proudest tree may be bowed, but not broken.' The daughters wept, and all eyes in the mansion had to be dried. Lady Daae had passed on—and I then passed on! Whew, whew, whew!

"I came again, as I often came across Fünen and the waters of the Belt, and rested near Borreby in the shelter of the beautiful oak forest. Here ospreys, wood pigeons, blue ravens, and even the black storks build their nests; it was the spring of the year, and some had eggs while others had even young ones. How they flew! How they cried! The sound of the ax could be heard, stroke after stroke; the trees were to be felled. Valdemar Daae had decided to build a ship, a great warship with three decks, which the king would surely buy, and for this the trees must fall and the birds lose their homes. The hawk flew away in terror as his nest was destroyed; the osprey and all the other birds flew around in terrified anger, screaming of their wrath and agony; I could understand them well enough. The crows and jackdaws shrieked in scorn, 'Caw, caw! From the nests!'

"And in the middle of the forest, with the workmen, stood Valdemar Daae and his three daughters, and they all laughed at the wild protests of the birds—all but the youngest, Anna Dorothea. She was a tenderhearted child, and when an old half-dead tree, on whose bare branches a black stork had built his nest, was to be cut down, it saddened her so to see the helpless young ones thrusting their heads out in the terror that she begged with tears in her eyes that this one tree be spared. So the tree with the black stork's nest was left standing.

"There was much hammering and sawing as the three-deck ship was being built. The master shipbuilder was a fine-looking young fellow, though of lowly birth, his eyes sparkling with life and his brow thoughtful. Valdemar Daae liked to hear him talk, and so did little Ide, his eldest daughter, who was now fifteen years old. And while he built the ship for her father, he built many a castle in the air besides, and saw himself and little Ide sitting there as man and wife. That might actually have come to pass if the castle had been of walled stone, with ramparts and moat, forest and gardens. But with all his skill, the builder was only a common bird, and what business did a sparrow have among a flock of cranes? Whew, whew, whew! I flew away and he flew away, and little Ide forgot it, as forget she must.

"In the stable the beautiful black horses neighed. They were worth looking at, and they were looked at. The admiral was sent by the king himself to inspect the new warship and to discuss buying it. He was loud in admiration for the splendid horses. I heard him well," said the Wind. "I followed the gentlemen through the open stable door and scattered about their feet wisps of straw, yellow as gold. Gold! That was what Valdemar Daae wanted, and the admiral wanted the black horses he admired so greatly, but all their discussion came to nothing. The horses weren't bought, and neither was the ship! It was left on the shore with planks over it, a Noah's ark that was never to float on water. Whew, whew, whew! It was a pity!

"In the winter, when the fields were covered with snow and ice floes choked the Belt," said the Wind, "flocks of black ravens and crows came and perched on the lifeless, solitary ship as it stood on the shore. The frantic old birds and the homeless young ones screamed hoarse tales about the oak forest that had been ravished and the many wonderful nests that had been destroyed, all for the sake of this great piece of useless lumber, the proud vessel that was never to sail the seas. And I tossed and whirled the snow about until it lay thickly over the ship;

I made it listen to my voice and taught it all that a storm has to say; I certainly did my part in teaching it all a ship should know of life. Whew, whew, whew! On, on, on!

"And winter passed away, winter and summer passed, as they always pass, as I pass, as the snow melts, as the leaf drifts downward, as the apple blossom fades, away, away, away! And as people pass away!

"But the daughters were still young. Little Ide was still as blooming a rose as when the shipbuilder had seen her. Often I caught hold of her long brown hair when she stood thoughtfully beside the apple tree in the garden, and she didn't notice that I shook petals down on her hair, loosening it, as she gazed at the crimson sunset and the streak of golden sky through the dark bushes and trees. Her sister Johanne was still like a lily, bright and slender, straight and tall, as stiff upon her stalk as her mother had been. She loved to linger in the great hall where the portraits of their ancestors hung; the ladies were painted wearing velvets and silk, with tiny, pearl-embroidered hats set on their braids; they were beautiful ladies, indeed; the men were shown in steel armor, or in stiff white ruffs and rich mantles lined with squirrel fur, their swords belted to their sides, not around their waists. Johanne often wondered how her own portrait would look on those same walls, and what her husband would look like. Yes, she thought about that, and talked about it to herself. I heard it as I whipped through the long gallery into the hall and whirled around again.

"Anna Dorothea, the pale hyacinth, was still a very quiet child of fourteen, with large, thoughtful blue eyes, and the smile of childhood still lingering on her lips. Even if I could have I would never have blown that smile away. I met her in the garden, in the narrow lane, or in the fields, gathering herbs and flowers for her father to use in the wondrous potions and mixtures he used to prepare.

"Valdemar Daae, though haughty and conceited, was also a man of skill and great knowledge. People knew that and spoke about it. Fire burned in summer as well as winter in the fireplace in his study; his chamber door was always locked; night and day he worked, yet he seldom spoke of his labors. He knew that the secrets of nature must be wooed secretly, and he was seeking the best secret of all—how to produce pure red gold!

"The smoke therefore rose out of the chimney continuously, and the fire crackled as it burned. I was there!" sang the Wind. "I whistled up the chimney. 'Stop it! Stop it!' I sang through the chimney. 'It will all end in smoke, dust, embers, and ashes! You will burn yourself up! Whew, whew! Stop it!' But Valdemar Daae did not stop.

"Those superb horses in the stable—what became of them? And the fine old gold and silver in cupboards and chests, the cattle in the meadows, the mansion and all its riches? Yes, they were all melted down in the gold-making crucible, and yet no gold came of it. Barn and granary, cellar and pantry, all were empty now; the house sheltered fewer folk and more mice. One windowpane was broken, another cracked," said the Wind, "and now I had no need to go around to the door to get in. The chimney still smoked, to be sure, not for cooking dinner, but for cooking the red gold.

"I blew through the courtyard gates, like the watchman blowing his horn, but there was no watchman here," said the Wind. "I whirled the weathercock round and round, and it creaked like the snoring of the watchman, but there was no watchman; only rats and mice were there; poverty loaded the table and stuffed wardrobe and larder; the doors sagged from their hinges; there were chinks and cracks in plenty, so that I could go in and out at will.

"In the smoke and ashes, beset by sorrow and sleepless nights, Valdemar's hair and beard turned gray; his skin grew coarse and yellowish; his eyes still looked greedily for gold—the long hoped-for gold!

"I blew ashes and smoke into his face and beard. I whistled through the broken panes and open cracks and blew into the daughters' chest of drawers, where they kept their clothes, which now were faded and threadbare from constant use, but which had to last them. The poor dears never had such a song as this sung at their cradles; but none, save I, sang any song at all in the great hall now. The life of abundance had turned into one of poverty," said the Wind. "I snowed them in, and it is said that snow puts one in a good humor. They had no firewood, for the forest was destroyed. There came a sharp frost, and while I sprang through holes and passages and over walls and roofs to keep myself warm, the highborn daughters huddled in bed against the cold, and their father crept beneath a covering of rude skins. Nothing to eat, nothing to burn!

"It was a hard lesson they had to learn!

"Whew, whew, whew! But Valdemar Daae couldn't learn. 'After winter comes the spring,' he said, 'and after troubles come the good times; we have only to wait, wait! Now the mansion is mortgaged! Now it is high time indeed—and so we shall have gold! By Easter!' And then I saw him watching a spider at work, and heard him mutter, 'Good, industrious little weaver, you teach me to persevere! Your web may be broken, but you only begin it again; again it may be torn asunder, but all undismayed you return again and again to your work, and you are rewarded at last!'

"Then Easter morning came, and the bells rang and the sun shone in the heavens. He had awakened in a feverish heat; he had boiled and seethed and distilled and compounded. I heard him sigh like a lost soul and I heard him pray; I felt that he was holding his breath. The lamp had gone out, but he did not notice it. I blew on the coals until a flame shone on his chalk-white face and lighted up those staring eyes. But then those eyes became larger and larger—until they seemed about to burst.

"Behold the alchemistic glass! It glittered, glowing, pure and heavy; he lifted it with faltering hand; he cried with stumbling tongue, 'Gold! Gold!' He staggered, dizzy, and I could have blown him down as he stood," said the Wind, "but I only blew on the live coals, then followed him through the door to where his daughters sat, shivering. Ashes sprinkled his beard, clung to his dress, and lay in his matted hair. He stood erect and lifted high his treasure in its fragile glass. 'I've found it! I've won!' he cried. 'Gold!' The glass flashed in the sunbeams as he held it high—and then, lo! his hand trembled so that the alchemistic glass fell to the floor and shivered into a thousand fragments! His last bubble had burst! Whew, whew, whew! On, on, on! And I went on, away from the alchemist's home.

"Toward the end of that year, during the short days when the mist flings wet drops on the red berries and leafless branches, I came back in happy spirits, swept the heavens clean, and broke off the dead branches; that is not very hard work, to be sure, but it has to be done. And at the same time there was a different sort of sweeping and cleaning out at Borreby Mansion. Valdemar Daae's old enemy, Ove Ramel of Basnaes, was there with the mortgage on the mansion and all its contents. I drummed on the broken panes, beat against the ruined doors, and whistled through the cracks and chinks; Master Ove shouldn't find it pleasant to stay there. Ide and Anna Dorothea wept quietly; Johanne stood pale and stately and bit her thumb till it bled; but all that did no good.

"Ove Ramel generously offered to allow Mr. Daae to remain at the mansion during his lifetime, but he got no thanks for the gesture. I listened, and noticed how the homeless old nobleman held his head more proudly than ever. I rushed against the mansion and the old lime trees, so that the thickest branch broke off—and it wasn't a rotten one, either. There it lay at the gate, like a broom for sweeping out—and there was sweeping out there, you may be sure! But I had expected it.

"Oh, that was a day of bitterness—a sorrowful day! But with a stiff neck and a stout back the proud man bore his burden bravely.

"They had nothing left except the clothes they wore, and the new alchemistic glass, filled with the brittle treasure that had promised so much—the fool's gold scraped up from the floor; this Valdemar Daae hid in his breast. He took his cane in his hand, and with his three daughters the once rich nobleman walked out of Borreby Mansion. I blew cold upon his flaming cheeks and stroked his gray beard and long white hair to and fro as I sang, as loudly as I could, "Whew, whew, whew! This was the end of his glory!

"Ide and Anne Dorothea walked on each side of him, but as Johanne crossed the threshold she turned back. Perhaps, as he gazed so wistfully at the red stones that had once made up Marsk Stig's castle, she remembered the old ballad about Marsk Stig's daughters:

The elder took the younger by the hand,
And forth they went to a distant land.

"Was she thinking of this song? Here were three daughters, and their father was with them. They turned off from the highway, where they had used to drive in their carriage, and made their way to Smidstrup Field, to a little shack of mud they had rented for ten marks a year. These bare walls and empty chambers were their new 'mansion.' Crows and jackdaws circled above their heads, screaming, as if in mockery, 'Turned out of the nest! Caw, Caw!' just as they had screamed in Borreby Wood when the oaks were being cut down. Mr. Daae and his daughters must have understood the cries; they were not pleasant to listen to, so I did my best to drown them out by blowing about their ears.

"Thus they passed into the shack of mud on Smidstrup Field, and I passed away over field and moor, through bare hedges and leafless woods, away over open waters, to other lands—whew, whew! On, on! Year after year!"

What happened to Valdemar Daae; what happened to his daughters? The Wind will tell us:

"The last time I went to see them I found only Anna Dorothea, the pale hyacinth. She was then old and bent; it was half a hundred years later. She had lived the longest; she knew the whole story.

"Across the heath, near the town of Viborg, there stood the dean's beautiful new house, with red stones and pointed gables and chimneys always smoking busily. The gentle lady and her beautiful daughters sat on the balcony and looked out over the hanging buckthorn in the garden, out to the brown heath; what did they look at there? They looked at the stork's nest on that dilapidated cottage out there. Houseleek and moss made up most of the roof, if one could call it a roof; the stork's nest covered the greater part of it, and that alone was in good condition, for the stork kept it that way.

"It was a house to look at but not to touch," said the Wind. "I had to pass by it very gently. The hut was left there only for the sake of the stork's nest, for it was a certainly no credit to the heath. The dean didn't want to drive the stork away, so the poor old woman who had lived in the hut had permission to stay there and shelter herself as well as he could. For that she owed thanks to the queer Egyptian bird; or was it because, so many years ago, she had pleaded for the nest of his wild black brother in Borreby Wood? Then she, the poor woman, was a happy child, a delicate, pale hyacinth in the garden of her ancestral home. She remembered it now; Anna Dorothea forgot nothing.

"'Oh!' she sighed—yes, humans can sigh almost like the Wind himself does among the reeds and rushes. 'Oh!—there were no bells to ring at your funeral, Valdemar Daae! No groups of poor schoolboys sang psalms when Borreby's former master was laid to rest! Oh, but everything comes to an end—misery as well as happiness! It grieved my father worst of all that my sister Ide should become the wife of a peasant, a miserable peasant whom he could have punished by making him ride a hard plank. But he is at peace in the grave now, and you are with him, Ide! Oh, yes, ah, me—I am still here. I am old and poor. Deliver me, kind Christ!'"

Such was the prayer of Anna Dorothea in the miserable mud hut that was allowed to stand only for the sake of the stork.

"The boldest and most resolute of the three sisters I carried off myself," said the Wind. "She cut her clothes like a man's, disguised herself as a poor lad, and went into service as a sailor. She was sparing of speech, cross-looking, but quick at her work, although she couldn't climb the mast. So one night I blew her overboard, before anyone found out she was a woman; and I think that was the right thing to do.

"It was another Easter morning, bright as that morning when Valdemar Daae thought he had found the gold. Among those tumbledown walls beneath the stork's nest I could hear a faint voice chanting a psalm. It was Anna Dorothea's last hymn.

"There was no window with glass, only a hole in the wall; but the sun set itself there like a lump of gold, and as she gazed on its glory her heart broke and her eyes grew fixed. The stork had given her shelter to the day of her death. I sang at her funeral," said the Wind, "as I had sung at her father's; I know where his grave is, and her grave, but no one else knows.

"Now there are new times, changed times. The old highway is lost in the fields, old cemeteries have been made into new roads, and soon the steam engine, with its row of cars, will come to rush over the forgotten graves of unknown ancestors. Whew, whew, whew! On, on!

"And that's the story of Valdemar Daae and his daughters; tell it better, you people, if you think you can," said the Wind, then veered around.

He was gone.

THE GIRL WHO TROD ON THE LOAF (1859)

You have quite likely heard of the girl who trod on a loaf so as not to soil her pretty shoes, and what misfortunes this brought upon her. The story has been written and printed, too.

She was a poor child, but proud and arrogant, and people said she had a bad disposition. When but a very little child, she found pleasure in catching flies, to pull off their wings and make creeping insects of them. And she used to stick May bugs and beetles on a pin, then put a green leaf or piece of paper close to their feet, so that the poor animals clung to it, and turned and twisted as they tried to get off the pin.

"The May bug is reading now," little Inger would say. "See how it turns the leaves!"

As she grew older she became even worse instead of better; but she was very pretty, and that was probably her misfortune. Because otherwise she would have been disciplined more than she was.

"You'll bring misfortune down upon you," said her own mother to her. "As a little child you often used to trample on my aprons; and when you're older I fear you'll trample on my heart."

And she really did.

Then she was sent into the country to be in the service of people of distinction. They treated her as kindly as if she had been their own child and dressed her so well that she looked extremely beautiful and became even more arrogant.

When she had been in their service for about a year, her mistress said to her, "You ought to go back and visit your parents, little Inger."

So she went, but only because she wanted to show them how fine she had become. But when she reached the village, and saw the young men and girls gossiping around the pond, and her mother sat resting herself on a stone nearby, with a bundle of firewood she had gathered in the forest, Inger turned away; she was ashamed that one dressed as smartly as she should have for a mother such a poor, ragged woman who gathered sticks for burning. It was without reluctance that she turned away; she was only annoyed.

Another half year went by.

"You must go home someday and visit your old parents, little Inger," said her mistress. "Here's a large loaf of white bread to take them. They'll be happy to see you again."

So Inger put on her best dress and her fine new shoes and lifted her skirt high and walked very carefully, so that her shoes would stay clean and neat, and for that no one could blame her. But when she came to where the path crossed over marshy ground, and there was a stretch of water and mud before her, she threw the bread into the mud, so that she could use it as a steppingstone and get across with dry shoes. But just as she placed one foot on the bread and lifted the other up, the loaf sank in deeper and deeper, carrying her down until she disappeared entirely, and nothing could be seen but a black, bubbling pool! That's the story.

But what became of her? She went down to the Marsh Woman, who brews down there. The Marsh Woman is an aunt of the elf maidens, who are very well known. There have been poems written about them and pictures painted of them, but nobody knows much about the Marsh Woman, except that when the meadows begin to reek in the summer the old woman is at her brewing down below. Little Inger sank into this brewery, and no one could stand it very long there. A cesspool is a wonderful palace compared with the Marsh Woman's brewery. Every vessel is reeking with horrible smells that would turn a human being faint, and they are packed closely together; but even if there were enough space between them to creep through, it would be impossible because of the slimy toads and the fat snakes that are creeping and slithering along. Into this place little Inger sank, and all the horrible, creeping mess was so icy cold that she shivered in every limb. She became more and more stiff, and the bread stuck fast to her, drawing her as an amber bead draws a slender thread.

The Marsh Woman was at home, for the brewery was being visited that day by the Devil and his great-grandmother, the latter a very poisonous old creature who was never idle. She never goes out without taking some needlework with her, and she had brought some this time. She was sewing bits of leather to put in people's shoes, so that they should have no rest. She embroidered lies, and worked up into mischief and slander thoughtless words that would otherwise have fallen harmlessly to the ground. Yes, she could sew, embroider, and weave, that old great-grandmother!

She saw Inger, then put on her spectacles and looked again at her. "That girl has talent," she said. "Let me have her as a souvenir of my visit here; she will make a suitable statue in my great-grandchildren's antechamber." And she was given to her!

Thus little Inger went to hell! People don't always go directly down there; they can go by a roundabout way, when they have the necessary talent.

It was an endless antechamber. It made one dizzy to look forward and dizzy to look backward, and there was a crowd of anxious, exhausted people waiting for the gates of mercy to be opened for them. They would have long to wait. Huge, hideous, fat spiders spun cobwebs, of thousands of years' lasting, over their feet, webs like foot screws or manacles, which held them like copper chains; besides this, every soul was filled with everlasting unrest, an unrest of torment and pain. The miser stood there, lamenting that he had forgotten the key to his money box. Yes, it would take too long to repeat all the tortures and troubles of that place.

Inger was tortured by standing like a statue; it was as if she were fastened to the ground by the loaf of bread.

"This is what comes of trying to have clean feet," she said to herself. "Look at them stare at me!"

Yes, they all stared at her, with evil passions glaring from their eyes, and spoke without a sound coming from their mouths. They were frightful to look at!

"It must be a pleasure to look at me," thought little Inger. "I have a pretty face and nice clothes." And then she turned her eyes; her neck was too stiff to move. My, how soiled she had become in the Marsh Woman's brewery! Her dress was covered with clots of nasty slime; a snake had wound itself in her hair and dangled over her neck; and from every fold of her dress an ugly toad peeped out, barking like an asthmatic lap dog. It was most disagreeable. "But all the others down here look horrible, too," was the only way she could console herself.

Worst of all was the dreadful hunger she felt. Could she

stoop down and break off a bit of the bread on which she was standing? No, her back had stiffened, her arms and hands had stiffened, her whole body was like a statue of stone. She could only roll her eyes, but these she could turn entirely around, so she could see behind her, and that was a horrid sight. Then the flies came and crept to and fro across her eyeballs. She blinked her eyes, but the flies did not fly away, for they could not; their wings had been pulled off, and they had become creeping insects. That was another torment added to the hunger, and at last it seemed to her as if part of her insides were eating itself up; she was so empty, so terribly empty.

"If this keeps up much longer, I won't be able to stand it!" she said.

But she had to stand it; her sufferings only increased.

Then a hot tear fell upon her forehead. It trickled over her face and neck, down to the bread at her feet. Then another tear fell, and many more followed. Who could be weeping for little Inger? Had she not a mother up there on Earth? A mother's tears of grief for her erring child always reach it, but they do not redeem; they only burn, and they make the pain greater. And this terrible hunger, and being unable to snatch a mouthful of the bread she trod underfoot! She finally had a feeling that everything inside her must have eaten itself up. She became like a thin, hollow reed, taking in every sound.

She could hear distinctly everything that was said about her on Earth above, and what she heard was harsh and evil. Though her mother wept sorrowfully, she still said, "Pride goes before a fall. It was your own ruin, Inger. How you have grieved your mother!" Her mother and everyone else up there knew about her sin, that she had trod upon the bread and had sunk and stayed down; the cowherd who had seen it all from the brow of the hill told them.

"How you have grieved your mother, Inger!" said the mother. "Yes, I expected this!"

"I wish I had never been born!" thought Inger. "I would have been much better off. My mother's tears cannot help me now."

She heard how her employers, the good people who had been like parents to her, spoke. "She was a sinful child," they said. "She did not value the gifts of our Lord, but trampled them underfoot. It will be hard for her to have the gates of mercy opened to let her in."

"They ought to have brought me up better," Inger thought. "They should have beaten the nonsense out of me, if I had any."

She heard that a song had been written about her, "the haughty girl who stepped on a loaf to keep her shoes clean," and was being sung from one end of the country to the other.

"Why should I have to suffer and be punished so severely for such a little thing?" she thought. "The others certainly should be punished for their sins, too! But then, of course, there would be many to punish. Oh, how I am suffering!"

Then her mind became even harder than her shell-like form.

"No one can ever improve in this company! And I don't want to be any better. Look at them glare at me!"

Her heart became harder and full of hatred for all mankind.

"Now they have something to talk about up there. Oh, how I am suffering!"

When she listened she could hear them telling her story to children as a warning, and the little ones called her "the wicked Inger." "She was so very nasty," they said, "so nasty that she deserved to be punished." The children had nothing but harsh words to speak of her.

But one day, when hunger and misery were gnawing at her hollow body, she heard her name mentioned and her story told to an innocent little girl, who burst into tears of pity for the haughty, clothes-loving Inger.

"But won't she ever come up again?" the child asked.

"She will never come up again," they answered her.

"But if she would ask forgiveness and promise never to be bad again?"

"But she will not ask forgiveness," they said.

"Oh, how I wish she would!" the little girl said in great distress. "I'd give my doll's house if she could come up! It's so dreadful for poor Inger!"

These words reached right down to Inger's heart and seemed almost to make her good. For this was the first time anyone had said, "Poor Inger," and not added anything about her faults. An innocent little child had wept and prayed for her, and she was so touched by it that she wanted to weep herself, but the tears would not come, and that was also a torture.

The years passed up there, but down below there was no change. Inger heard fewer words from above; there was less talk about her. At last one day she heard a deep sigh, and the cry, "Inger, Inger, how miserable you have made me! I knew that you would!" Those were the dying words of her mother.

She heard her name mentioned now and then by her former mistress, and it was in the mildest way that she spoke: "I wonder if I will ever see you again, Inger! One never knows where one is to go!" But Inger knew that her kindly mistress would never descend to the place where she was.

Again a long time passed, slowly and bitterly. Then Inger heard her name again, and she beheld above her what seemed to be two bright stars shining down on her. They were two mild eyes that were closing on earth. So many years had passed since a little girl had wept over "Poor Inger" that that child had become an old woman, now being called by the Lord to himself. At that last hour, when the thoughts and deeds of a lifetime pass in review, she remembered very clearly how, as a tiny child, she had wept over the sad story of Inger. That time and that sorrow were so intensely in the old woman's mind at the moment of death that she cried with all her heart, "My Lord, have I not often, like poor Inger, trampled underfoot your blessed gifts and counted them of no value? Have I not often been guilty of the sin of pride and vanity in my inmost heart? But in your mercy you did not let me sink into the abyss, but did sustain me! Oh, forsake me not in my final hour!"

Then the old woman's eyes closed, but the eyes of her soul were opened to things formerly hidden; and as Inger had been so vividly present in her last thoughts she could see the poor girl, see how deeply she had sunk. And at that dreadful sight the gentle soul burst into tears; in the Kingdom of Heaven itself she stood like a child and wept for the fate of the unhappy Inger. Her tears and prayers came like an echo down to the hollow, empty shape that held the imprisoned, tortured soul. And that soul was overwhelmed by all that unexpected love from above. One of God's angels wept for her! Why was this granted her?

The tormented soul gathered into one thought all the deeds of its earthly life, and trembled with tears, such tears as Inger had never wept before. Grief filled her whole being. And as in deepest humility she thought that for her the gates of mercy would never be opened, a brilliant ray penetrated down into the abyss to her; it was a ray more powerful than the sunbeams that melt the snowmen that boys make in their yards. And under this ray, more swiftly than the snowflake falling upon a child's warm lips melts into a drop of water, the petrified figure of Inger evaporated; then a tiny bird arose and followed the zigzag path of the ray up to the world of mankind.

But it seemed terrified and shy of all about it; as if ashamed and wishing to avoid all living creatures, it hastily concealed itself in a dark hole in a crumbling wall. There it sat trembling all over, and could utter no sound, for it had no voice. It sat for a long time before it dared to peer out and gaze at the beauty about; yes, there was beauty indeed. The air was so fresh and soft; the moon shone so clearly; the trees and flowers were so fragrant; and the bird sat in such comfort, with feathers clean and dainty. How all creation spoke of love and beauty! The bird wanted to sing out the thoughts that filled its breast, but it could not; gladly would it have sung like the nightingale or the cuckoo in the springtime. Our Lord, who hears the voiceless hymn of praise even from a worm, understood the psalm of thanksgiving that swelled in the heart of the bird, as the psalm echoed in the heart of David before it took shape in words.

For weeks these mute feelings of gratitude increased. Someday surely they would find a voice, perhaps with the first stroke of the wing performing some good deed. Could not this happen?

Now came the feast of holy Christmas. Close by the wall a farmer set up a pole and tied an unthreshed bundle of oats on it, that the fowls of the air might also have a merry Christmas, and a joyous meal in this, the day of our Savior.

Brightly the sun rose that Christmas morning and shone down upon the oats and all the chirping birds that gathered around the pole. Then from the wall there came a faint "tweet, tweet." The swelling thoughts had at last found a voice, and the tiny sound was a whole song of joy as the bird flew forth from its hiding place; in the realm of Heaven they well knew who this bird was.

The winter was unusually severe. The ponds were frozen over thickly; the birds and wild creatures of the forest had very little food. The tiny bird flew about the country roads, and whenever it chanced to find a few grains of corn fallen in the ruts made by the sleds, it would eat but a single grain itself, while calling the other hungry birds, that they might have some food. Then it would fly into the towns and search closely, and wherever kindly hands had strewed bread crumbs outside the windows for the birds, it would eat only a single crumb and give all the rest away.

By the end of the winter the bird had found and given away so many crumbs of bread that they would have equaled in weight the loaf upon which little Inger had stepped to keep her fine shoes from being soiled; and when it had found and given away the last crumb, the gray wings of the bird suddenly became white and expanded.

"Look, there flies a sea swallow over the sea!" the children said as they saw the white bird. Now it seemed to dip into the water; now it rose into the bright sunshine; it gleamed in the air; it was not possible to see what became of it; they said that it flew straight into the sun.

OLE, THE TOWER KEEPER (1859)

In this world things go up and down and down and up!" said Ole, the tower keeper. "Now I can't get any higher! Up and down and down and up; that's the fate of most of us; in fact, we all become tower keepers at last; we look at life and things from above."

Thus spoke my friend Ole, in his tower—a chatty, jolly fellow who seemed to say whatever came into his head yet had so many serious thoughts concealed deep in his heart. He came from a good family; there were some who said that he was a conference councillor's son, or might have been. He had a good education, had been the assistant to a schoolmaster, the deputy of a parish clerk, but what help could that have been! When he lived with the parish clerk it was agreed that he should have free use of everything in the house. He was then young and a bit of a dandy as we call it, and he wanted shoe polish to brush and shine his boots with; but the parish clerk would only allow him grease, and so they had a quarrel. One spoke of stinginess, the other of vanity; the shoe polish became the black cause of their strife, and so they separated.

But what he wanted from the parish clerk he wanted of the world generally—the very best polish, and he always got its substitute, grease, so he turned his back on everybody and finally became a hermit. But in a big city, hermitage with a livelihood is to be found only in the church tower, so up it he went, and there he would smoke his pipe and pace up and down on his lonely walks, looking upward and downward, and talking in his own way about what he saw or didn't see, what he read in books or in himself.

I often lent him books to read, good books, for by the company one keeps shall he be known. He didn't care for the English-governess type of novel, he said, nor for the French ones, either, which he called a brew of empty wind and rose stalks; no, he liked biographies and books about the wonders of nature. I visited him at least once a year, generally soon after the new year; he always had something to tell which the change of year suggested to his thoughts.

I shall tell about two visits, and use his own words as far as I can.

FIRST VISIT

Among the books I had recently lent Ole was one about pebbles, which had greatly pleased him.

"They are truly veterans from olden times, those pebbles," he said, "yet people pass them by without thinking, and trample them down in fields or on beaches, those fragments of antiquity. I have done so myself. From now on I shall hold every paving stone in high respect! Thank you for the book; it has driven cobwebby old thoughts and ideas out of my head and made me eager to read more of the same type.

"The romance of the Earth is truly the most fascinating of all romances. It's a shame we can't read the first parts of it; but they're written in a language we haven't learned yet; we have to dig away among strata and rocks, puzzling out bits here and there from the early acts of earth's drama. The acting persons of the drama, old Mr. Adam and Mrs. Eve, don't make their entrance before the sixth act; that's far too late for many impatient readers, who want them to come on stage right away, but it's all the same to me. It is indeed a most marvelous romance, and here we are all in it. We creep and crawl about, but always stay where we are, while all the while the globe keeps turning around, but never splashing its ocean spray over us. The crust on which we move remains solid so that we never fall through, and so it is a story of millions of years, with steady progress.

"Many thanks for your book on pebbles; those old fellows could tell us so much if only they could talk. Isn't it funny to be a nobody once in a while, like me, and then remember that we all, whether we have the best shoe blacking or not, are just like tiny ants on the anthill of the world, even though some of us ants have stars and decorations, honors and offices? And it makes you feel so ridiculously young, compared with the millions of years of these venerable stones! I read your book on New Year's Eve and became so lost in it that I entirely forgot my usual New Year's Eve entertainment—watching the wild hunt to Amager; but you don't know what that is.

"The witches' flight to the Blocksberg on Midsummer Eve is, of course, well known, but we also have a wild mob, in this land and in our time, which speeds to Amager on New Year's Eve. All the bad poets, poetesses, newspaper hack writers, musicians, and artistic lions who are not worth anything else ride through the air to Amager on New Year's Eve. They sit astride their pencils or quill pens—for steel pens are too stiff for riding. I watch them every New Year's Eve—I could name most of them, but it isn't worthwhile—they don't imagine that anybody knows of their trip through the air on the quill pens. There is a sort of a niece of mine who is a fisherwoman and writes scandal and slander for three respectable papers; she says she has been out there as an invited guest, and they carried her, for since she cannot herself use a pen she couldn't ride on one. She has described the whole affair. Half of what she told me is probably a lie, but the other half is enough.

"When she was well underway they all broke into song; each of the guests had written his own song, and each sang his own composition, because, of course, he thought it was the best. They were all very much alike; and all sung to the same melody. Then, in little groups, up marched those who occupy themselves only as chatterboxes. They were now singing bells that sang alternately. Then came the small drummers, who drummed in family groups. Those who write anonymously were introduced—those, let me say here, whose grease is used for shoe polishing. There was the executioner, and his helper, and the helper was the worst, for otherwise no one would have paid any attention to him. There was the street sweeper with his cart, who turns over his dustbin and calls it "good, very good, remarkably good." During all this merriment, such as it was, there would shoot forth from holes scattered about now a gaunt stalk, now a leafless tree, a huge flower, or a large mushroom, and finally a roof that bore upon itself everything this honorable assembly had given to the world during the preceding year. Bright sparks could be seen glittering among them—there were the borrowed thoughts they had used, which now cut themselves loose and flew up like fireworks.

"A game called 'the stick burns' was played; and the younger poets played 'heartburns.' The jesters told their jokes, and the jokes rang out like empty pots being thrown against doors. My niece said it was most amusing; she told me a good deal more, too malicious to mention, but very funny. So you see, since I know so much about this midnight festival, it's only natural I should be interested in watching for it every New Year's Eve.

"But this year I forgot all about it. I was rolling through millions of years with my rocks, watching them break loose up in the North, drift along on icebergs ages before the building of Noah's ark, sink to the bottom of the sea, then mount again on a reef, and at last peer up through the water and say, 'This shall be Zealand!' I saw them become the homes of many different birds whose species we don't know, and the homes of savage chieftains we don't know either, until the ax hewed out in runic letters the names of a few that can thus take a place in our histories. I had gone beyond all lapse of time and had become a nonentity.

"Then three or four beautiful shooting stars fell; they shone brightly, and started my thoughts off in an entirely different direction. Does anybody know what a shooting star really is? The learned do not know! But I have my own idea about them, and this is it:

"How often is it that not a single word of thanks or blessing is given for a generous action or beautiful work that rejoices all who witness it! Yes, often that gratitude is voiceless, but still it doesn't fall wasted to the ground. I can fancy it is caught up by the sunshine, and eventually the sunbeams carry it away and shower it over the head of the benefactor. Sometimes the thanks of a whole nation are thus due; they may come late, but at last they do come like a bouquet, when a shooting stars falls over the grave of some hero or statesman. Thus it's a great thrill to me when I see a shooting star, especially on New Year's Eve, and try to guess for whom that bouquet of gratitude can be meant. A short time ago a radiant shooting star fell in the southwest—now for whom could that have been intended? I am sure it fell right over the bank by the Flensborg Fjord, where the white-crossed flag of Denmark floats over the graves of Schleppegrell, Laessoe, and their comrades. Another one fell in the heart of Zealand, fell upon Sorö; I'm sure that was a bouquet for Holberg's grave, a thanksgiving from the multitude who during years past have laughed over his delightful plays.

"It is a great thought, a happy thought, to know that a shooting star like that will fall upon our own graves! Well, none will ever fall on mine; no sunbeam will bring me thanks, for I haven't done anything to be thanked for. I don't even merit polish for my boots," said Ole. "My lot in life has been only to get grease."

SECOND VISIT

On another New Year's Day I went to the tower, and this time Ole talked about the "Skaal" toasts that had been drunk with the change of the old year to the new. Then he gave his story of the glasses, and there was sense in what he said.

"On New Year's Eve when the clock strikes twelve, people rise from the table with freshly filled glasses and drink a toast to the new year. So people begin the new year with a glass in their hands, and that's fine for people who like to drink; others start the year by going to bed, and that's first rate for lazybones! But then, sleep is sure to play a leading part in the coming year, and so is the glass.

"Do you know what lives in the glasses?" he asked. "Why, health, happiness, and joy live there! Misfortune and bitter misery dwell there! When I count up the glasses I can tell the gradations of the different people.

"You see, the first glass is the glass of health. In it grows the health herb. Stick that into your beam, and by the end of the year you may sit in the arbor of health.

"Now take the second glass. Ah, yes, out of it there flies a little bird, singing with such innocent happiness that men listen to it and perhaps sing with it, 'Life is beautiful! We will not hang our heads! Put cheer and courage forth!'

"From the third glass a tiny winged imp darts out. You can't call him a little angel, for he has the blood and soul of a goblin, all for jest and mischief. He lurks behind our ear and whispers some queer drollery; he creeps into our heart and warms it until one becomes frolicsome, becomes the great wit in a party of wits.

"In the fourth glass there is neither herb, nor bird, nor fairy. That glass is the boundary line of sense, beyond which you should never, never pass.

"Do you take the fifth glass? Then will you weep over yourself, or laugh with a fierce shout. For out of this glass will spring riotous Prince Carnival, flippant and wild as an elf. He will overcome you, until you forget your dignity, if you ever had any, and forget things you ought not to forget. All is dance and song and revelry; the masks carry you away with them, and the daughters of evil, in silk and flowers, come with flowing hair and alluring charms. Tear yourself loose if you can!

"And the sixth glass! Yes, in that sits Satan himself, a little, well-dressed charming man who never contradicts you, tells you that you are always right. He comes with a lantern to guide you home! What sort of home, and what sorts of spirits live there? There's an old legend about a saint who was ordered to choose one of the seven deadly sins, and chose what he thought was the least—drunkenness. But in it he committed all the other six. Man and the Devil mixed with blood—that is the sixth glass; and all the evil seeds within us thrive on it, and each of them sprouts with a force like the grain of mustard, in the Bible, and grows into a mighty tree, spreading out over the whole world.

"Most have nothing before them but to be put into the smelting oven and be cast in a new mold.

"This is the story of the glasses," said Ole, the tower keeper, "and it can be told both with shoe polish and grease! I give it to you with both."

That was my second visit to Ole. If you want to hear more, we will have to pay him another visit.

ANNE LISBETH
(1859)

Anne Lisbeth's complexion was like peaches and cream; her eyes were bright, her teeth shiny white; she was young, gay, and beautiful to look upon; her steps were light and her mind was even lighter. What would come of all this? "That awful brat," people said about her baby; and indeed he wasn't pretty, so he was left with the ditchdigger's wife.

Anne Lisbeth went into service in the count's castle. There she sat in a magnificent room, dressed in silk and velvet; not a breath of wind was allowed to blow on her nor anyone to speak a harsh word to her. She was nurse to the count's child, who was as beloved as a prince, beautiful as an angel. How she loved him!

Her own child was provided for in the ditchdigger's house, where his wife's temper boiled over more often than her pot. Sometimes the child was left alone all day long, and cried; but what nobody hears doesn't bother anyone! He cried himself to sleep, and in sleep there is neither hunger nor thirst; sleep is such a good invention!

"Ill weeds grow fast," says the proverb, and Anne Lisbeth's boy did indeed shoot up rapidly. It was as if he had taken root in the ditchdigger's household; his mother had paid for his up-bringing and considered herself well rid of him. She was a city lady now, was well provided for, and whenever she went out she was beautifully dressed; but she never went to see her son at the ditchdigger's; that was too far from the city, and there was no reason for her to go there, anyway; the boy was theirs, and now, they decided, it was time for him to earn his keep; so he found work tending Mads Jensen's red cow.

The watchdog at Blegdam Manor sits proudly on top of its house in the sunshine, barking at passersby, but in rainy weather it lies, warm and dry, inside its kennel. Anne Lisbeth's boy sat at the edge of a ditch in the sunshine, whittling sticks or watching three blossoming strawberry plants; he hoped they would soon turn into berries—that was his happiest thought—but the berries never ripened. Through sunshine or showers he sat there; he was often soaked to the skin, but the cold wind soon dried his clothes on his body. Whenever he went to the farmyard he received only kicks and cuffs and was called "stupid and ugly"; he was used to that—nobody loved him.

How did Anne Lisbeth's boy get along? How could he under such circumstances? It was his fate never to be loved.

At last he was literally pushed off the earth and sent to sea in a wretched little sailing vessel. Here he took the helm while the skipper drank—a frostbitten, shabby-looking little boy, and always hungry! One would think he never had enough to eat, and that really was the case.

It was late in the autumn, wet, raw, stormy weather, with a wind that cut through the warmest clothing, especially out at sea. A miserable little vessel with one sail drove on before the wind; it had a crew of two men, or rather a man and a half—the skipper and his boy. All day the light had been no brighter than twilight; now it grew still darker and it was bitterly cold. The skipper brought forth a bottle and a glass and took a swallow to warm himself up; the top of the glass was whole, but its foot had been broken off, so instead it had a little piece of wood, painted blue, to stand on. A drink is a great comfort, and two are even better. The boy was at the helm, holding it with rough, tarred hands, a wretched, shrinking form with unkempt hair; it was the ditchdigger's boy, registered in the parish records as the son of Anne Lisbeth.

The wind drove the ship hard before it; the sail bellied out before the power of the wind; it was rough and wet everywhere, and it might soon be even worse. Stop! What was that? What crashed? What sprang up? What grasped the little vessel? The boat whirled around. Was it a waterspout or a tidal wave? The boy at the helm screamed, "Lord Jesus, save us!" The vessel had struck on a great rock, and it sank like a waterlogged old shoe in a duckpond; sank with "man and mouse," as the saying goes; there were mice on board, but only a man and a half—the skipper and the ditchdigger's boy. No one saw it, save the screaming gulls above and the darting fishes beneath, and these hardly saw it clearly, for they fled in terror when the water poured into the doomed vessel. There it lay, scarcely a fathom below the water, and the two were drowned and forgotten. Only the glass was left, for the blue wooden block kept it afloat, and it drifted onto the shore. Where and when? That is of no consequence. That old broken glass had been useful, and had been loved, too, in a way; which Anne Lisbeth's son had never been. However, in the Kingdom of Heaven no soul shall ever have cause to sigh, "Never loved!"

Anne Lisbeth meanwhile had been living for several years in a large town; she was addressed as "madam" and always held herself very proudly when she spoke of olden times, of the times when she rode in a carriage and talked with countesses and baronesses. And she talked of her foster child, that sweetest of little angels, and how he had loved her and she had loved him, how they had kissed and caressed each other, for he was her pride and joy. Now he was tall, fourteen years old, a bright, beautiful boy. She hadn't seen him since the time she carried him in her arms; for many years she had not been at the count's castle, which was a long journey away.

"But I must find a way to get there someday," said Anne Lisbeth. "I must see my sweet young count again. He must be missing me, and loving me as he did when his angelic little arms clung around my neck and he said, 'Ann-Lis,' as sweet as a violin. Ah, yes, I must make short work of it and see him again!"

So she made the long trip, partly on foot and partly by wagon. The castle was as magnificent and the gardens as lovely as ever, but the servants were all new to her, and not one of them knew Anne Lisbeth or what she had once meant there. But the countess would tell them, she thought, and her own boy; how she longed for him!

Now Anne Lisbeth was finally here, but they kept her waiting a long time. At last, just before the household went to dinner, she was called in. The countess spoke to her very courteously and promised that after dinner she should see her beloved boy. So she had to wait for another summons.

How tall, thin, and lanky he had grown, but he still had his beautiful eyes and angelic mouth; and he looked straight at her without a word. Certainly he had no recollection of her. He turned to go, but she caught his hand and pressed it to her lips. "All right," he said, "that's enough," and then he left the room.

The ungrateful young nobleman, whom she had loved above all on Earth and had made the pride of her life!

So Anne Lisbeth left the castle and made her way homeward along the highway. She was very sorrowful; he had been so cold and strange to her, without a word or thought for her, he whom she had once carried in her arms night and day and always had carried in her heart.

Then a huge black raven flew down and alighted on the road just in front of her and croaked again and again. "Oh, what bird of ill omen are you?" she said.

As she passed the ditchdigger's house, his wife was standing in the doorway, and they spoke to one another.

"How robust you look!" said the ditchdigger's wife. "You are plump and stout! Everything must be going well with you."

"Pretty well," replied Anne Lisbeth.

"The boat went down with them," said the ditchdigger's wife. "Skipper Lars and your boy were both drowned. So that ends that. But I hoped that the boy would have lived to help me out from time to time with a little money; he hasn't cost you anything for a long while, you know, Anne Lisbeth."

"Drowned, are they?" repeated Anne Lisbeth, and then said nothing more on that subject.

Anne Lisbeth was heartsick because the young count wouldn't speak to her, she who loved him so and had taken that long trip to see him; the journey had also been expensive. The pleasure it had brought her was little indeed. But she didn't say a word about it; she wouldn't lighten her mind by talking about it to the ditchdigger's wife, who might think she was no longer welcome at the count's castle. While they were talking, the raven again flew screaming over her head. "That ugly black thing!" said Anne Lisbeth. "That's the second time it's frightened me today!"

She had brought some coffee beans and chicory with her; it would be a kindness to the ditchdigger's wife to give these to her and share a cup with her. While the old woman went to make the coffee Anne Lisbeth sat down and soon fell asleep.

Strangely enough, she dreamed of one whom she had never seen in her dreams before—her own child, who in that very house had hungered and wept, who had been kicked about in heat and cold, and who now lay deep below the sea, the good Lord only knew where. She dreamed that even as she sat there waiting for the coffee and smelling the fragrance drifting in to her from the kitchen, a shining little angel, beautiful as the young count, stood in the doorway and spoke to her.

"The end of the world is come," said the little angel. "Hold fast to me, for you are still my mother! You have an angel in Paradise. Hold fast to me!" Then he took hold of her, and at that very moment there came a tremendous crash, as though the whole world were bursting into pieces, and as the angel rose in the air, holding her tightly by her sleeves, she felt herself lifted from the ground. But then something heavy clung to her feet and dragged her down; it was as if a hundred other women were holding tightly to her, screaming, "If you are to be saved, we must be saved, too! Hold fast! Hold fast!" And then they all clung to her. The weight was too heavy; ritsch, ratsch!—her sleeves were split, and she fell down in terror—and awoke.

Her head was so dizzy she nearly fell off the chair where she was sitting. She could not understand her dream clearly, but she felt it foretold evil for her.

They had their coffee and talked for a while. Then Anne Lisbeth walked on to the nearest village, where she was to meet the carrier and drive home with him that evening. But when she got there, the carrier told her he couldn't start until the following evening. She thought it over—what it would cost her to stay there, the length of the distance home, and realized that if she went along the seashore instead of by road, it would be nearly two miles shorter; it was clear weather and the moon was at the full. And so Anne Lisbeth decided to go at once; she could be home the next day.

The sun had set, the vesper bells were still ringing—no, it was not the bells, but Peter Oxe's frogs croaking in their pond. Soon they, too, were silent, and then all was still; no bird raised its voice, for all were at rest; and it seemed the owl was not at home. The hush of death settled over forest and shore. She could hear her own footsteps in the sand. No wave disturbed the sea, the deep waters were at peace; everywhere was silence, silence among the living and the dead.

Anne Lisbeth walked on, not thinking of anything in particular, as we say. Yet, though she was not conscious of it, her thoughts were busy within her, as they always are within all of us. They lie asleep inside us, thoughts that have already shaped themselves into action and thoughts that have never yet stirred—there they lie still, and someday they will come forth. It is written: "The labor of righteousness is peace;" and again it is written: "The wages of sin are death!" Much has been said and written that one does not know—or, as it was with Anne Lisbeth, does not remember—but such things can appear before one's subconscious self, can come to mind, though one is unaware of it.

The germs of vices and virtues are alive deep in our hearts—in yours and mine; they lurk like tiny invisible seeds. There comes a ray of sunshine or the touch of an evil hand; you turn to the right or to the left, and the little seed quivers into life, puts forth shoots, and pours its life throughout all the veins. Walking in a daydream, one may be unconscious of many painful thoughts, but they have their being within us all the same; thus Anne Lisbeth walked as if in a daydream, but her thoughts lived within her.

From Candlemas to Candlemas the heart has much written upon it, even the record of the whole year. Many sins are forgotten, sins in word or thought, sins against God or our neighbor or our own conscience; we think not of them, nor did Anne Lisbeth. She had broken no laws of the land; she knew that she was popular, esteemed, even respected.

Now, as she walked along the shore, suddenly something made her start and stand still! What was it? Only an old man's hat. Where could that have been washed overboard? She drew closer and looked down at it.

Oh! What was that lying over there? She became very frightened, and yet it was nothing but a heap of tangled seaweed, but to her fancy it had seemed for a moment the body of a man. As she continued on her way she remembered many stories she had heard as a child about the old superstitious belief in the "sea ghost"—the ghost of a drowned body that lay still unburied, washed by the tides on the wild seashore. The lifeless body itself could harm no one, but the "sea ghost" would follow a solitary wanderer, clinging fast to him and demanding to be carried to the churchyard and buried in consecrated ground. "Hold on! Hold on!" it would cry; and as Anne

Lisbeth thought of these words, all at once there came back to her most vividly her dream—how the mothers had clung to her, screaming, "Hold fast! Hold on!" how the world had split beneath her, how her sleeves had been torn apart and she had fallen from the grasp of her child, who had tried to hold her up in the hour of doom. Her child, her own flesh and blood, whom she had never loved and scarcely ever thought of, was now lying at the bottom of the sea; any day his body might be washed ashore, and his ghost might follow her, wailing, "Hold on! Hold on! Bury me in Christian earth!"

Panic-stricken by this horrible thought, she ran faster and faster. Terror touched her heart with a cold, clammy finger; she was ready to faint. And as she looked upon the sea, the air grew thicker and thicker, a heavy mist fell over the scene, veiling tree and bush in strange disguises. She turned to seek for the Moon behind her—and it was only a pale disk without rays. Then something heavy seemed to drag at her limbs; "Hold on! Hold on!" she thought. And when she again turned toward the Moon its white face seemed close beside her, and the mist hung like a shroud over her shoulders. "Hold on! Bury me in Christian earth!"—she could almost hear those words. And then she did hear a sound, so hollow, so hoarse—not the voices of the frogs in the pond nor the tones of the raven, for neither was nearby, but clearly she heard the dreadful words, "Bury me! Bury me!" Yes! It was, it must be, the ghost of her own child, who could find no rest for his soul until his body was carried to the churchyard and laid in a Christian grave.

To the churchyard she would hurry; that very hour she would dig the grave; and as she turned toward the church her burden seemed to grow lighter, until it disappeared altogether.

As soon as she felt that, she started back to follow the short cut to her home, but once more her limbs sank beneath her, and again the terrible words rang in her ears, "Hold on! Hold on!" It sounded like the croaking of a frog and like a wailing bird.

"Bury me! Bury me!"

Cold and clammy was the mist, but still colder and clammier were her hands and face under the touch of fear! A heavy weight again clung to her and seemed to drag her down; her heart quaked with thoughts and feelings that had never stirred within her before this moment.

In our northern countries a single spring night is often enough to dress the beech wood, and in the morning sunlight it appears in its young, bright foliage.

In one second the seed of sin within us may be lifted to the light and unfolded into thoughts, words, and deeds; and thus it is when conscience is awakened. And our Lord awakens it when we lest expect it; when there is no way to excuse ourselves, the deed stands open to view, bearing witness against us; thoughts spring into words, and words ring clearly throughout the world. Then we are horrified to find what we have carried within us, that we have not overcome the evil we have sown in thoughtlessness and pride. The heart hides within itself all vices and virtues, and they grow even in the shallowest ground.

Anne Lisbeth, overwhelmed with the realization of her sin, sank to the ground and crept along for some distance. "Bury me! Bury me!" still rang in her ears, and gladly would she have buried herself, if the grave could have brought eternal forgetfulness. It was her hour of awakening, and she was full of anguish and horror; superstition made her blood run hot and cold. Many things of which she had feared to speak came into her mind. There passed before her, silently as a shadowy cloud in the clear moonlight, a vision she had heard of before. It was a glowing chariot of fire, drawn by four snorting horses, with fire blazing from their eyes and nostrils; and inside sat a wicked nobleman who more than a century ago had ruled here. Every midnight, he rode into his courtyard and right out again. He was not pale, like other ghosts; no, his face was as black as burnt coal. As he passed Anne Lisbeth he nodded and beckoned to her, "Hold on! Hold on! You may ride in a count's carriage once more and forget your child."

She pulled herself together and hastened to the churchyard, but the black crosses and the black ravens mingled before her eyes; the ravens screamed as they had done that morning, but now she could understand what they were saying. "I am Mother Raven! I am Mother Raven!" said each of them, and Anne Lisbeth knew the name fitted herself well; maybe she would be changed into a huge black bird like these, and have to cry as they cried, if she did not dig the grave.

Then she flung herself on the ground and began frantically digging with her hands in the hard earth; she dug till the blood ran from her fingers.

"Bury me! Bury me!" Still she heard those words, and every moment she dreaded to hear the cock crow and see the first streak of dawn in the east. For if her task were not completed before daylight she knew she would be lost.

And the cock did crow, and the light appeared in the east— and the grave was only half dug, and behold! An icy hand slid over her head and face, down to her heart. A voice seemed to sigh, "Only half the grave!" and a shadowy form drifted past her and down to the bottom of the ocean. Yes, it was indeed the "sea ghost," and Anne Lisbeth fell fainting to the earth, exhausted and overpowered, and her senses left her.

When she came to, it was bright daylight, and two men were lifting her up. She was lying not in the churchyard, but down on the seashore, where she had been digging a deep hole in the sand, and had cut her fingers on a broken glass, the stem of which was stuck in a wooden block painted blue.

Anne Lisbeth was ill; her conscience had spoken loudly to her that night, and superstitious terror had mingled its voice with the voice of conscience. She had no power to distinguish between them; she was now convinced that she had but half a soul, while the other half had been borne away by her child, away to the bottom of the ocean; and never could she hope for the mercy of God until she again possessed the half soul that was imprisoned in those deep waters.

Anne Lisbeth went home, but she was no longer the same. Her thoughts were like tangled yarn; there was only one thread that she could clearly grasp; just one idea possessed her, that she must carry the "sea ghost" to the churchyard and there dig a grave for it. Many a night they missed her from her home and always found her down by the shore, waiting for the "sea ghost." So a whole year passed, and then one night she disappeared and this time was sought in vain. All of the following day was spent in searching for her.

Toward evening, when the parish clerk entered the church to ring the bell for vespers, he found Anne Lisbeth lying before the altar. She had been here ever since dawn; her strength was nearly gone, but her eyes were bright and a faint rosy hue lighted her face; the last sunbeams shone down upon her, streamed over the altar, and glowed on the bright silver clasps of the Bible, open at this text from the Prophet Joel; "Rend your heart and not your garments, and turn unto the Lord your God." This was just by chance, said people, as so many things happen by chance.

In Anne Lisbeth's face, as the setting sun shone upon it, were peace and grace. Now she was so happy, she said. Now she had won back her soul! During the past night the spirit of her own child had been with her and had said, "You dug but half a grave for me, but now for a year and a day you have entombed me in your own heart, and that is the only proper resting place a mother can provide for her child!" And then he had returned to her lost half soul and guided her to the church!

"Now I am in God's house!" she said. "And only there can one be happy!"

When the sun had set, the soul of Anne Lisbeth had gone way up from this Earth to where there are no fears nor the troubles that we have here, even such as those of Anne Lisbeth.

THE CHILD IN THE GRAVE (1859)

There was sorrow in the house; there was sorrow in every heart, for the youngest child, a four-year-old boy, the joy and future hope of his parents, was dead. They had two older daughters, the eldest of whom was to be confirmed that year; sweet, good girls, they both were; but the child one has lost is always the most precious, and this was not only the youngest but the only son. It was indeed a heavy affliction. The sisters grieved as the young grieve, awed by the sorrow of their parents; the father's head bowed in grief; but most of all the mother suffered.

Night and day she had cared for the sick child, nursed it, carried it with her, guarded it constantly until it was a part of herself. She could not conceive that he was dead, that he should be laid in a coffin and rest in a dark grave. God would never take her child from her, she thought; when it happened, however, and was a certainty, she cried aloud in her agony, "God had known nothing of this! He has heartless servants here upon earth; they do as they like and pay no heed to the prayers of a mother!"

In her grief she turned from God, and then came dark thoughts, thoughts of death, everlasting death—that human beings became earth in the Earth and that all was over.

Her words were bitter, for her heart was black with despair. There were hours when she could not even find solace of tears; she had no thought for her young daughters; she never looked up at her husband when his tears fell on her hot forehead; her thoughts were all with her dead child; her mind could recall only cherished memories of him—his winning ways, his innocent, childish prattle.

The day of the funeral came. For several nights she had not closed her eyes; but early in the morning of this day, overcome at last by weariness, she fell asleep. And during her sleep the coffin was carried into a distant room and there the lid was nailed down, so that she would not hear the sound of the hammering.

When she awoke she demanded to see her child, but her husband replied through his tears, "We have closed the coffin; it had to be done."

"When God deals cruelly with me," she cried, "why should people treat me better!" And then she was overcome with bitter tears.

The coffin was carried to the grave; the inconsolable mother sat with her young daughters, but she looked at them without seeing them, for her thoughts had nothing more to do with her home. She resigned herself to sorrow, and it tossed her to and fro as the sea tosses the rudderless ship. Thus passed the day of the funeral, and several days followed, all dark with the same heavy monotony of sorrow. Her family watched her with moist eyes and sorrowful glances; she did not heed their words of comfort. What comfort could they offer when they themselves were grieving?

It seemed to her as though she would never sleep again, yet sleep could be her best friend; it could strengthen her body and bring rest to her embittered soul. They persuaded her to lie down, and she would lie in her bed as quietly as though she were actually sleeping.

One night her husband listened to her steady breathing and really thought that at last she had found repose. With folded hands he thanked God, and soon fell into a sound, deep sleep. So he was not aware that his wife rose, dressed herself, and went quietly out of the house, to seek the spot where her thoughts were night and day, the grave that hid her child. She walked through the garden and into the field beyond, where a footpath led to the churchyard. Nobody saw her, and she saw no one.

It was a beautiful, starry night in early September; the air was mild. She entered the churchyard, and when she reached the little grave it was like one huge bouquet of fragrant flowers. She sat there and bowed her head over the grave, as if she could see through the thick covering of earth the dear child whose smile she so well remembered, that adoring look in the sweet eyes as she bent over his sickbed and lifted the tiny hand he had no strength to raise. And as then she sat beside his bed, now she sat beside his grave, but here her tears flowed freely and fell upon the grave.

"You wish to go down to your child!" said a voice close to her, a voice so clear, so profound, it resounded in her heart. She looked up, and there standing beside her was a figure shrouded in a heavy black mourning cloak. Over the head spread a hood, yet she could see the face beneath it, and that stern face inspired trust; those grave eyes sparkled with the light of youth.

"Down to my child!" she repeated in a sad, pleading tone, like a despairing prayer.

"Do you dare to follow me?" asked the figure. "I am Death!"

And she bowed her head in silent assent. Suddenly each of the millions of stars above shone with the brightness of the full moon; she beheld the richly colored splendor of the flowers on the grave, while the earth covering it yielded gently and softly like a waving cloth. She sank, and the black mantle of Death was spread over her, and all was darkness; she sank deeper than the spade of the gravedigger can reach, until the churchyard lay like a roof above her head.

The black folds of the mantle fell aside, and she was standing in a mighty hall that was as friendly as it was big; there was a twilight all around. Before her appeared her child, and in the same moment she held him close to her heart. He smiled at her and looked more beautiful than ever before; she uttered a cry, which, however, was inaudible, for just then the hall was filled with music, now swelling high and triumphant, now dying away into tones faint but clear. Such blessed sounds had never before reached her ears; they seemed to come from beyond the heavy black curtain that divided the hall from the great land of eternity.

"My sweet mother! My own mother!" she heard her child say. It was the familiar, beloved voice; and kiss followed kiss in boundless happiness. Then the child pointed to the black curtain. "Look, Mother! There is nothing as beautiful as this on earth! Do you see, Mother? Do you see them all? This is happiness!"

But the mother could see nothing where the child pointed, nothing but the blackness of night; she gazed with earthly eyes and could not see as could the child whom God had called to himself. So it was with the music; she could hear the sounds, the tones, but not the words, the words in which she was to believe.

"I can fly now, Mother!" said the child. "Fly, with all the other happy children, straight into God's Paradise! Oh, I love that, but when you cry as you are crying now it calls me back, and I can no longer fly, and I want so much to. Will you not let me? You will join me here in only a little time, dearest Mother!"

"Oh, stay, stay!" she begged. "Only for a moment longer! Let me look at you once more, kiss you again, hold you fast in my arms!"

And she kissed him, holding him tightly. Suddenly she heard her name called from far overhead, called in a sad, imploring tone! What could it mean?

"Don't you hear?" said the child. "It is Father calling you!"

And a few seconds later she heard deep sighs, which sounded as if they came from weeping children. "They are my sisters!" said the child. "Oh, Mother, surely you have not forgotten them!"

And now she remembered the beloved ones she had left in her home, and a great fear swept over her. She looked around her and saw the different forms that were continually gliding past, to disappear behind the black curtain. She imagined she recognized some of them; could her husband or her little girls be among them? No, their cries, their sighs, had come from far above her; she had nearly forgotten them for the dead.

"Mother," said the child, "the bells of Paradise are ringing! The sun is rising!"

Then an overpowering light streamed out on her—and the child was gone, and she herself was carried upward. Then all was cold around her, and when she lifted her head she found herself lying on her child's grave in the churchyard. But in her dream the Lord had become a rest for her foot, a light for her understanding. She sank to her knees and prayed, "O my Lord, forgive me that I wished to keep an immortal spirit from its flight into eternity and could forget my duties toward the living ones you have given me here!"

And with that prayer it seemed as if her heart at last found relief.

The sun came out, a little bird sang above her, and the church bells began to ring for the morning service. Light was all about her; light was once more in her heart; she felt the goodness of God and remembered her duties as, longing, she hurried to her home. There she bent over her husband, and her warm, tender kiss awakened him, and they could speak together of their loss. Now she was strong and calm, as a wife should be, and from her lips came words of trust and confidence. "God's will is always best."

"Where did you so suddenly gain this strength," her husband asked her, "this comfort?"

Then she kissed him and kissed her daughters. "It came to me from God, by the grave of my child!"

TWO BROTHERS (1859)

On one of the Danish islands, where old thingsteads, the judgment seats of our forefathers, loom up in the cornfields and mighty trees raise their heads above the beech forests, there lies a little town of low houses with red roofs. In one of these houses strange things were being prepared on the open stove, over the coals and embers. There was boiling in test tubes, mixing and distilling, and pounding of drugs in mortars. An elderly man was in charge of everything.

"One must be careful and do the right thing," he said. "Yes, the right, the correct thing; the truth in each created thing, we must recognize and keep hold of."

In the living room sat the mother with her two sons—still young, with mature thoughts. Their mother had always taught them about right and reason and to hold fast to truth, which she said is the face of God in this world.

The elder of the boys looked bright and alert; he liked to read about the forces of nature, of suns and stars—no fairy tale could give him greater joy. Oh, how wonderful to be able to go on voyages of discovery, or to discover how to imitate birds' wings and fly! Yes, these were the great things to find! Father was right and Mother was right; truth holds the world together.

The younger brother was more quiet and lived entirely in his books. If he read of Jacob, and how he clad himself in sheep-skins to resemble Esau and thus cheat him of his birthright, the boy would clench his tiny fists in anger against the deceiver. If he read of tyrants and of all the injustice and wickedness that reigned in the world, tears would come into his eyes. Thoughts of the right, the truth that should and someday would triumph, moved him profoundly.

One evening, the little boy was already in bed, but the curtains were not drawn about him and the light shone in on him. He lay there with his book, eager to finish reading the history of Solon.

Then his thoughts lifted him and carried him strangely on, as if his bed had changed into a vessel under sail—was he dreaming? Or what else could it mean? He was gliding over rolling waves, across the great ocean of time; and he heard the voice of Solon, proclaiming in his foreign tongue, which the boy could still understand, the motto of Denmark—"By law the land is built!"

Then the Genius of the human race stood in that humble room, bent down over the bed, and kissed the boy on his forehead. "Be strong in fame and strong in the battle of life! With truth in your heart fly toward the land of truth!"

The older brother was not yet in bed; he stood at the window, gazing out at mists arising from the meadow. They were not elf maidens dancing out there, as an honest old servant had told him; he knew much more about it. They were vapors, warmer than the air, and that is why they rose. A shooting star lit up the sky, and the boy's thoughts went instantly from the vapors of the earth way up into the regions of the shining meteor.

The stars of Heaven twinkled; it was as if long threads of gold were floating from them down on our Earth.

"Fly with me!" it sang and rang in the boy's heart. The mighty Genius of mankind carried him up, far swifter than bird or arrow or any flying thing of Earth, out into space, where ray after ray from star to star bound all the globes together; Earth was spinning in the thin air and cities seemed to lie close to each other. Through the spheres it sounded: "What is near and what is far, while the mighty genius of thought lifts you on high?"

And again the boy was at the window, gazing out, while the younger brother lay abed; and their mother called them by their names, "Anders and Hans Christian!"

Denmark knows both those two brothers—the world knows them—Oersted!

PEN AND INKSTAND (1859)

In a poet's study, somebody made a remark as he looked at the inkstand that was standing on the table: "It's strange what can come out of that inkstand! I wonder what the next thing will be. Yes, it's strange!"

"That it is!" said the Inkstand. "It's unbelievable, that's what I have always said." The Inkstand was speaking to the Pen and to everything else on the table that could hear it. "It's really amazing what comes out of me! Almost incredible! I actually don't know myself what will come next when that person starts to dip into me. One drop from me is enough for half a piece of paper, and what may not be on it then? I am something quite remarkable. All the works of this poet come from me. These living characters, whom people think they recognize, these deep emotions, that gay humor, the charming descriptions of nature—I don't understand those myself, because I don't know anything about nature—all of that is in me. From me have come out, and still come out, that host of lovely maidens and brave knights on snorting steeds. The fact is, I assure you, I don't know anything about them myself."

"You are right about that," said the Pen. "You have very few ideas, and don't bother about thinking much at all. If you did take the trouble to think, you would understand that nothing comes out of you except a liquid. You just supply me with the means of putting down on paper what I have in me; that's what I write with. It's the pen that does the writing. Nobody doubts that, and most people know as much about poetry as an old inkstand!"

"You haven't had much experience," retorted the Inkstand. "You've hardly been in service a week, and already you're half worn out. Do you imagine you're the poet? Why, you're only a servant; I have had a great many like you before you came, some from the goose family and some of English make. I'm familiar with both quill pens and steel pens. Yes, I've had a great many in my service, and I'll have many more when the man who goes through the motions for me comes to write down what he gets from me. I'd be much interested in knowing what will be the next thing he gets from me."

"Inkpot!" cried the Pen.

Late that evening the Poet came home. He had been at a concert, had heard a splendid violinist, and was quite thrilled with his marvelous performance. From his instrument he had drawn a golden river of melody. Sometimes it had sounded like the gentle murmur of rippling water drops, wonderful pearl-like tones, sometimes like a chorus of twittering birds, sometimes like a tempest tearing through mighty forests of pine. The Poet had fancied he heard his own heart weep, but in tones as sweet as the gentle voice of a woman. It seemed as if the music came not only from the strings of the violin, but from its sounding board, its pegs, its very bridge. It was amazing! The selection had been extremely difficult, but it had seemed as if the bow were wandering over the strings merely in play. The performance was so easy that an ignorant listener might have thought he could do it himself. The violin seemed to sound, and the bow to play, of their own accord, and one forgot the master who directed them, giving them life and soul.

Yes, the master was forgotten, but the Poet remembered him. He repeated his name and wrote down his thoughts.

"How foolish it would be for the violin and bow to boast of their achievements! And yet we human beings often do so. Poets, artists, scientists, generals—we are all proud of ourselves, and yet we're only instruments in the hands of our Lord! To him alone be the glory! We have nothing to be arrogant about."

Yes, that is what the Poet wrote down, and he titled his essay "The Master and the Instruments."

"That ought to hold you, madam," said the Pen, when the two were alone again. "Did you hear him read aloud what I had written?"

"Yes, I heard what I gave you to write," said the Inkstand. "It was meant for you and your conceit. It's strange that you can't tell when anyone is making fun of you. I gave you a pretty sharp cut there; surely I must know my own satire!"

"Inkpot!" said the Pen.

"Scribble-stick!" said the Inkstand.

They were both satisfied with their answers, and it is a great comfort to feel that one has made a witty reply—one sleeps better afterward. So they both went to sleep.

But the Poet didn't sleep. His thoughts rushed forth like the violin's tones, falling like pearls, sweeping on like a storm through the forest. He understood the sentiments of his own heart; he caught a ray of the light from the everlasting Master.

To him alone be the glory!

THE FARMYARD COCK AND THE WEATHERCOCK (1859)

Once there were two cocks, one on a dunghill and one on the roof, both of them conceited; but which of the two did the most? Tell us what you think—we'll keep our own opinion, anyway.

The chicken yard was separated by a board fence from another yard, where there lay a manure heap, and on this grew a great cucumber, which was fully aware of being a forcing—bed plant.

"That's a privilege of birth," said the Cucumber to herself. "Not everyone can be born a cucumber; there must be other living things, too. The fowls, the ducks, and the cattle in the next yard are creatures, too, I suppose. I now look up to the Farmyard Cock on the fence. He certainly is much more important than the Weathercock way up there, who can't even creak, much less crow, who has no hens or chickens, who thinks only about himself and perspires rust. No, the Farmyard Cock—he's a real cock! His walk is like a dance, to hear him crow is like music, and whenever he comes around people can hear what a trumpeter he is! If he would only come over here! Even if he should eat me up, stalk and all, it would be a happy death!" said the Cucumber.

That night the weather turned very bad. The hens and chickens and even the Cock himself sought shelter. The wind blew down the fence between the two yards with a terrific crash; tiles fell from the roof, but the Weathercock sat firm. He didn't even turn around, because he couldn't. Although he was young and just cast he was very steady and sedate. He had been "born old," and wasn't a bit like the sparrows and swallows that fly through the vault of heaven. He despised them: "Ordinary piping birds of no importance!" he called them. He admitted that the pigeons were big and glossy, and gleamed like mother-of-pearl, and almost looked like some kind of weathercock, but then they were fat and stupid, and all they could think of was stuff themselves with food.

"Besides, they're such terrible bores to associate with," said the Weathercock.

The migratory birds had also visited the Weathercock and told him tales of foreign lands—of caravans in the sky and fierce robber stories of encounters with birds of prey—and that was new and interesting the first time, but the Weathercock knew that afterward they kept repeating themselves, and that became monotonous.

"They're boring, and everything is dull. Nobody's fit to associate with; all of them are tiresome and dull. The world is no good!" he said. "The whole thing is a bore!"

The Weathercock was what you might call blasé, and that would certainly have made him interesting to the Cucumber if she had known about it; but she had eyes only for the Farmyard Cock, who had now come into her own yard.

The wind had blown down the fence, but the lightning and the thunder were over.

"How's that for crowing? the Farmyard Cock said to his hens and chicks. "It was a little rough perhaps—not elegant enough."

And the hens and chickens picked at the manure heap, while

the Cock strutted to and fro on it like a knight.

"Garden plant!" he said to the Cucumber; and with that word she understood his great importance and forgot that he was pecking at her and eating her up—a happy death!

Then the hens came and the chickens came, for when one of them runs somewhere the rest run, too; they clucked and chirped and gazed at the Cock and were proud that he belonged to them.

"Cock-a-doodle-doo!" he crowed. "The chickens will immediately grow up to be fine large fowls if I make a noise like that in the chicken yard of the world!"

And the hens and chickens answered him with their clucking and their chirping. And then the Cock told them a great piece of news. "A cock can lay an egg, and do you know what that egg has inside it? In that egg there's a basilisk. But no one can stand the sight of a basilisk. People know that, and now you know it, too—you know what's in me, and what a wonderful fellow I am!"

With that the Farmyard Cock flapped his wings, swelled up his comb, and crowed again. All the hens shivered, and the little chickens shivered, but they were tremendously proud that one of their kind should be such a cock of the world. They clucked and they chirped until the Weathercock could hear it; he heard it, but he never moved.

"It's all stupid nonsense!" said a voice within the Weathercock. "The Farmyard Cock never lays eggs, and I'm too lazy to do it. If I wanted to I could lay a wind egg; but the world isn't worth a wind egg. It's all stupid nonsense. And now I don't even want to sit here any longer."

With that the Weathercock broke off; but he didn't fall on

the Farmyard Cock and kill him, "although he intended to!" said the hens. And what's the moral of this? "It is better to crow than to be 'stuck-up' and break off!"

"BEAUTIFUL" (1859)

Alfred the sculptor—yes, you know him, don't you? We all know him; he was awarded the gold medal, traveled to Italy, and came home again. He was young then; in fact, he is still young, though he is ten years older than he was at that time.

After he returned home, he visited one of the little provincial towns on the island of Zealand. The whole village knew who the stranger was, and in his honor one of the richest families gave a party. Everyone of any importance or owning any property was invited. It was quite an event, and all the village knew about it without its being announced by the town crier. Apprentice boys and the children of poor people, and even some of their parents, stood outside the house, looking at the lighted windows with their drawn curtains; and the watchman could imagine that he was giving the party, there were so many people in his street. There was an air of festivity everywhere, and inside the house, too, for Mr. Alfred the sculptor was there.

He talked and told stories, and everybody listened to him with pleasure and enthusiasm, but none more so than the elderly widow of a state official. As far as Mr. Alfred was concerned, she was like a blank sheet of gray blotting paper, absorbing everything that was said and demanding more. She was highly susceptible and unbelievably ignorant—a sort of female Kaspar Hauser.

"I should love to see Rome!" she said. "It must be a wonderful city, with all the many strangers continually arriving there.

Now, do tell us what Rome is like. How does the city look when you come in by the gate?"

"It is not easy to describe it," said the young sculptor. "There's a great open place, and in the middle of it there is an obelisk that is four thousand years old."

"An organist!" cried the lady, who had never heard the word "obelisk."

Some of the guests could hardly keep from laughing, among them the sculptor, but the smile that rose to his lips quickly faded away, for he saw, close by the lady, a pair of dark-blue eyes; they belonged to the daughter of the lady who had been talking, and anyone with such a daughter could not really be silly! The mother was like a fountain of questions, and the daughter, who listened silently, might pass for the naiad of the fountain. How beautiful she was! She was something for a sculptor to look at, but not to speak with, for indeed she talked but very little.

"Has the Pope a large family?" asked the lady.

And the young man answered considerately, as if the question had been put differently, "No, he doesn't come of a very great family."

"That's not what I mean," said the lady. "I mean, does he have a wife and children?"

"The Pope isn't allowed to marry," he replied.

"I don't approve of that," said the lady.

She might well have talked and questioned him more intelligently, but if she hadn't said and asked what she did, would her daughter have leaned so gracefully on her shoulder, looking straight before her with an almost melancholy smile on her lips?

And Mr. Alfred told them of the glorious colors of Italy, the purple of the mountains, the blue of the Mediterranean, the blue of the southern skies, a beauty that could only be surpassed in the north by the deep-blue eyes of a maiden. This he said with peculiar meaning, but she who should have understood it looked quite unconscious, and that, too, was charming!

"Ah, Italy!" sighed some of the guests.

"Traveling!" sighed others.

"Charming, charming!"

"Well," said the widow, "if I win fifty thousand dollars in the lottery, we'll travel! My daughter and I. You Mr. Alfred, must be our guide. We'll all three go, with just one or two good friends with us." Then she smiled in such a friendly manner at the company that each of them could imagine he was the person who would accompany them to Italy. "Yes, we'll go to Italy! But not to the parts where the robbers are; we'll stay in Rome and only travel by the great highways where we'll be safe."

And the daughter sighed very gently. And how much may lie in one little sigh or be read into it! The young man read a great deal into it. Those two blue eyes, bright that evening in his honor, must conceal treasures of heart and mind rarer than all the glories of Rome! When he left the party, he had lost his heart—lost it completely—to the young lady.

Now, the widow's house was where Mr. Alfred the sculptor could most frequently be found. It was understood that his calls were not for the lady herself, though he and she did all the talking; he really came for the sake of the daughter. They called her Kala. Her real name was Karen Malene, but the two names had been contracted into the single name Kala. She was extremely beautiful, but some people said she was rather dull and probably slept late in the mornings.

"She has been accustomed to that since childhood," said her mother. "She is as beautiful as Venus, and a beauty always tires easily. She does sleep rather late, but that's what makes her eyes so bright."

What a power there was in these clear eyes, these deep blue eyes! "Still waters run deep." The young man felt the truth of that proverb, and his heart sank into the depths. He spoke of his adventures, and Mamma always asked the same naïve and pertinent questions she had asked at their first meeting.

It was a delight to hear Mr. Alfred speak. He told them of Naples, of trips to Mount Vesuvius, and showed them colored prints of some of the eruptions. The widow had never heard of such things before, much less taken time to think about them.

"Mercy save us!" she said. "So that's a burning mountain! But isn't it dangerous for the people who live there?"

"Entire cities have been destroyed," he answered. "For example, Pompeii and Herculaneum."

"Oh, the poor people! And you saw all that yourself?"

"Well, no, I didn't see any of the eruptions shown in these pictures, but I'll show you a drawing I made of an eruption I did see."

He laid a pencil sketch on the table, and when Mamma, who had been studying the highly colored prints, glanced at the black-and-white drawing, she cried in amazement, "When you saw it did it throw up white fire?"

For a moment Alfred's respect for Kala's mamma nearly vanished; but then, dazzled by the light from Kala, he decided it was natural for the old lady to have no eye for color. After all, it didn't matter, for Kala's mamma had the most wonderful thing of all—she had Kala herself.

And Alfred and Kala were engaged, which was inevitable, and the engagement was announced in the town newspaper. Mamma brought thirty copies of the paper, so she could cut out the announcement and send it to her friends. The betrothed couple were happy, and the mamma-in-law-to-be was happy, too; she said it seemed like being related to Thorvaldsen himself.

"At any rate, you are his successor," she told Alfred.

And it seemed to Alfred that Mamma had this time really said something clever. Kala said nothing, but her eyes sparkled; her every gesture was graceful. Yes, she was beautiful; that cannot be repeated too often.

Alfred made busts of Kala and his future mamma-in-law; they sat for him and watched how he molded and smoothed the soft clay between his fingers.

"I suppose it's only for us that you do this common work," said Mamma-in-law-to-be, "and don't have your servant do all that dabbing together."

"No, I have to mold the clay myself," he explained.

"Oh, yes, you're always so exceedingly polite," said Mamma, while Kala silently pressed his hand, still soiled by the clay.

Then he unfolded to both of them the loveliness of nature in creation, explaining how the living stood higher in the scale than the dead, how the plant was above the mineral, the animal above the plant, and man above the animal, how mind and beauty are united in outward form, and how it was the task of the sculptor to seize that beauty and imprison it in his works.

Kala sat silent and nodded approval of the thought, while

Mamma-in-law confessed, "It's hard to follow all that. But my thoughts manage to hobble slowly along after you; they whirl around, but I try to hold them fast."

And the power of Kala's beauty held Alfred fast, seizing him and mastering him and filling his whole soul. There was beauty in Kala's every feature; it sparkled in her eyes, lurked in the corners of her mouth and even in each movement of her fingers. The sculptor saw this; he spoke only of her, thought only of her, until the two became one. Thus it might be said that she also spoke often, for he was always talking of her, and they two were one.

Such was the betrothal; and now came the wedding day, with bridesmaids and presents, all duly mentioned in the wedding speech.

Mamma-in-law had set up a bust of Thorvaldsen, attired in a dressing gown, at one end of the table, for it was her whim that he was to be a guest. There were songs and toasts, for it was a gay wedding and they were a handsome pair. "Pygmalion gets his Galatea," one of the songs said.

"That is something from mythology!" said Mamma-in-law.

Next day the young couple left for Copenhagen, where they were to live. Mamma-in-law went with them, "to give them a helping hand," she explained—which meant to take charge of the house. Kala was to live in a doll's house. Everything was so bright, new, and fine. There the three of them sat, and as for Alfred, to use a proverb that describes his circumstances, he sat like the bishop in the goose yard.

The magic of form had fascinated him. He had regarded the case and had no interest in learning what the case contained, and that is unfortunate, very unfortunate, in married life! If the case breaks and the gilding rubs off, the purchaser may repent of his bargain. It is very embarrassing to discover in a large party that one's suspender buttons are coming off and that one has no belt to fall back on; but it is still worse to realize at a great party that one's wife and mother-in-law are talking nonsense and that one cannot think of a clever piece of wit to cover up the stupidity of it.

The young couple often sat hand in hand, he speaking and she letting drop a word now and then—with always the same melody, like a clock striking the same two or three notes constantly. It was really a mental relief when one of her friends, Sophie, came to visit them.

Sophie wasn't pretty. To be sure, she was not deformed; Kala always said she was a little crooked, but no one but a female friend would have noticed that. She was a very level-headed girl and had no idea that she might ever become dangerous here. Her visits brought a fresh breath of air into the doll's house, air that they all agreed was certainly needed there. But they felt they needed more airing, so they came out into the air, and Mamma-in-law and the young couple traveled to Italy.

"Thank Heaven we are back in our own home again!" said both mother and daughter when they and Alfred returned home a year later.

"Traveling is no fun," said Mamma-in-law. "On the contrary, it's very tiring; pardon me for saying so. I found the time dragged, even though I had my children with me; and it is expensive, very expensive, to travel. All those galleries you have to see, and all the things you have to look at! You must do it for self-protection, because when you get back people are sure to ask you about them; and then they're sure to tell you that you've missed the most worthwhile things. I got so tired at last of those everlasting Madonnas; I thought I would turn into a Madonna myself!"

"And the food one gets!" said Kala.

"Yes," agreed Mamma. "Not even a dish of honest meat soup! It is awful the way they cook!"

And Kala had become tired from traveling; she was always tired; that was the trouble. Sophie came to live with them, and her presence was a real help.

Mamma-in-law had to admit that Sophie understood both housekeeping and art, though you would hardly have expected a knowledge of the last from a person of her modest background. Moreover, she was honest and loyal; she showed that clearly when Kala lay sick, fading away.

If the case is everything, that case should be strong, or it is all over. And it was all over with the case—Kala died.

"She was so beautiful," said Mamma. "She was very different from the antiques, because they're all so damaged. Kala was completely perfect, just as a beauty should be."

Alfred wept and the mother wept, and both went into mourning. The black dresses became Mamma very well, so she wore her mourning the longer. Moreover, she soon experienced another grief, when she saw Alfred marry again. And he married Sophie, who had no looks at all!

"He has gone from one extreme to the other!" said Mamma-in-law. "Gone from the most beautiful to the ugliest! How could he forget his first wife! Men have no constancy. Now, my husband was entirely different, and he died before I did."

"Pygmalion got his Galatea," said Alfred. "Yes, that's what

the wedding song said. I really fell in love with a beautiful statue, which came to life in my arms, but the soulmate that Heaven sends down to us, one of its angels who can comfort and sympathize with and uplift us, I have not found or won till now. You came to me, Sophie, not in the glory of superficial beauty—but fair enough, prettier than was necessary. The most important thing is still the most important. You came to teach a sculptor that his work is only clay and dust, only the outward form in a fabric that passes away, and that we must seek the spirit within. Poor Kala! Ours was but a wayfarer's life. In the next world, where we shall come together through sympathy, we shall probably be half strangers to each other."

"That was not spoken kindly," said Sophie, "not like a true Christian. In the next world, where there is no marriage, but where, as you say, souls find each other through sympathy, where everything beautiful is developed and elevated, her soul may attain such completeness that it may resound far more melodiously than mine. Then you will again utter the first exciting cry of your love, 'Beautiful, beautiful!'"

A STORY FROM THE SAND DUNES (1859)

This is a story of the sand dunes of Jutland, but it doesn't begin there; no, it begins far away to the south, in Spain. The ocean is the highway between the two countries. So now let your thoughts journey to Spain!

It is warm there, and it is beautiful. The fiery red pomegranate blossoms grow among the dark laurels; a refreshing wind from the mountains breathes over the orange gardens and the graceful Moorish palaces with golden cupolas and colored walls. Children walk in procession through the streets, carrying torches and waving banners, while high above them stars sparkle in the clear arching vault of heaven. Song and castanets can be heard; young men and girls dance under the blossoming acacias, while the beggar lies on a carved marble block, quenches his thirst with a juicy watermelon, and dozes his life away. It is all like a beautiful dream; give yourself up to it. Yes, as did the young married couple to whom had been granted all the choicest of earthly blessings—health, beauty, good nature, riches, and honor.

"We are as happy as anyone could ever be!" they said, with full conviction in their hearts. Yet they had one step higher to go to attain complete happiness, and that would be reached when God would give them a child, a son in their own image, body and soul. That blessed child would be welcomed with jubilance, cared for with the utmost love and tenderness, and be surrounded by all the luxuries that riches and an influential family can provide.

Meanwhile the days glided past, each like a holiday.

"Life is a precious gift of love, almost too great to understand," said the wife. "And just to think that this fullness of bliss shall still increase and grow, in another life, throughout eternity. I can hardly conceive of it!"

"And it certainly also shows the arrogance of people," said her husband. "It really shows a terrible conceit when people persuade themselves to think they'll live forever—become as God! Were these not the words of the serpent, the master of lies?"

"You surely don't doubt that there is a life after this, do you?" asked his young wife, and it was as if a shadow passed through their sunlit thoughts for the first time.

"Faith promises it, I know, and the priests tell us it is so," said the young man. "But, happy as I am now, I feel and know that it is only pride, an arrogant thought that demands another life after this—an extension of this happiness. Haven't we been granted enough in this life, so that we could and should be satisfied?"

"Yes, that has been given us," said the young wife, "but how many thousands find this life a heavy trail! How many have been thrown into this world only to find poverty, shame, sickness, and misfortune! No, if there were no afterlife, the blessings on this Earth would be too unequally divided—our God would not be a God of justice!"

"The beggar down on the street has pleasures just as dear to him as the king enjoys in his splendid palace," said the young man. "And what about the poor beast of burden that is beaten and starved and works itself to death? Doesn't it sense the bitterness of its miserable life? Why shouldn't it too demand an afterlife, and call it unfair that it wasn't granted the advantages of a higher creation?"

"Christ told us, 'In my Father's house are many mansions,'" answered the young wife. "The Kingdom of Heaven is as infinite as God's love. The animal is His creation too, and I don't believe that any single life will be lost, but that each will be granted the greatest share of happiness it is capable of receiving."

"But this world is good enough for me now," said the young man, as he slipped his arm around his lovely, amiable wife and smoked a cigarette on the open balcony, where the cool air was heavy with the fragrance of orange blossoms and carnations. Songs and the clicking of castanets came from the street, while the stars glittered high above, and two eyes full of love—his wife's eyes—gazed on him with the expression of eternal love. "A moment like this," he said, "makes being born well worthwhile—just to experience such a moment—and then vanish," he said smiling, while his wife shook her finger reprovingly. And the cloud soon passed; they were much too happy.

Everything that happened seemed only to add to their happiness and well-being. A change came, but it was only a change of place, not a change that diminished their happiness and enjoyment of life. The young man was appointed by the king to be ambassador to the court of imperial Russia, a post of great honor, such as his birth and ability well fitted him to occupy. He had a great fortune of his own, and his young wife's wealth was equal to his, for she was the daughter of the richest and most respected merchant. And since one of her father's largest and finest ships would sail this year to Stockholm, it was arranged that the dear children, the daughter and the son-in-law, would travel on it to St. Petersburg. Everything was royally fitted out for the voyage, with soft carpets underfoot and silken splendor everywhere.

There is an old heroic ballad familiar to all Danes, called "The King of England's Son." He also goes to sea in a splendid ship, with its anchor inlaid with pure gold and every rope woven of silk. The ship of the Spanish merchant might have reminded one of this vessel, for the magnificence was similar, and the farewell thoughts were very much the same:

God grant that we meet with joy again!

The parting was brief, for a fair wind blew briskly off the Spanish coast. They hoped to reach their destination in a few weeks. But as soon as they were well out at sea the wind died down to rest. The ocean grew smooth, and the waters reflected the glittering light of the stars of heaven. There were festive evenings in their richly appointed cabin.

At last they wished the wind would rise again, to speed them on their voyage. But every wind that arose came from the wrong direction. Weeks went by; two whole months passed, in fact, before the wind blew in their favor, from the southwest.

They were somewhere between Scotland and Jutland when the west wind burst forth, just as in the old ballad, "The King of England's Son":

While the sky was dark and the wind blew,
And there was neither port nor land in view,
They cast their anchor, but to no avail;
They were blown to Denmark by a west wind gale.

This occurred a long time ago. King Christian VII, still a

young man, then sat on the throne of Denmark. Much has happened since then; there have been many changes and innovations. Lakes and swamps have become green meadows, while heaths have been plowed into useful land. And in the shelter of the West Jutlander's house there now grow apple trees and roses, but you must seek these out, for they hide from the sharp west wind.

Still, it is easy to imagine yourself back in times more remote than even the reign of Christian VII, for now, as then, the brown heath of Jutland stretches for miles with its barrows, its mirages, its winding, rough, sandy roads. To the west, where broad streams of water flow into the fjords, there are marshes and meadows, encircled by the high sand hills which rise up toward the sea like an Alpine chain with jagged summits, broken only by high banks of clay. From these the waves eat off giant mouthfuls year after year, so that the edges and summits topple down as though shaken by an earthquake. That's how it looks today, and that's how it looked many years ago, when the happy couple sailed past it in their splendid ship.

It was a bright, sunshiny Sunday in late September; the peals of the church bells extended to one another all along the Nissum Fjord. The churches there are like immense stones, each like a piece of rock mountain; the North Sea itself might wash over them, and they would still stand firm. Most of them have no towers, their bells hanging out in the open air between two wooden beams.

The services had ended, and the congregation emerged from the house of God into the churchyard where then, as now, there grew neither tree nor shrub. No plants, flowers, or wreaths adorned the graves; only rough hillocks showed where the dead had been buried, while sharp grass, beaten flat by the wind, covered the whole cemetery. Here and there a single grave still has a tombstone, perhaps a moldering log, cut in the shape of a coffin. These are pieces of driftwood from the forests of West Jutland. The wild sea provides the shore dwellers with many hewn planks, cast upon the coast. But the wind and salt sea spray soon wear away these monuments.

One of these blocks had been placed on the grave of child, to which a young woman came from the church. She stopped and gazed down at the rotted wood; shortly her husband joined her. They spoke no word; presently he took her hand, and together they walked away from the grave, on over the brown heath and over the moor toward the sand dunes. For a long time they walked in silence.

"That was a good sermon today," said the man. "If we didn't have our Lord we would have nothing."

"Yes," replied his wife, "He sends us happiness and sorrow. He has a right to. Our little boy would have been five years old tomorrow if we had been allowed to keep him."

"It does no good to grieve," said the man. "He is much better off there than here; he is where we pray to go."

They said no more, but passed on silently toward their home among the sand dunes. Suddenly, from one of these, where there was no grass to hold the sand down, it looked as if a column of heavy smoke were rising; it was really a gust of wind boring into the bank and whirling the fine particles of sand into the air. A second gust followed, so strong that the strings of fish hung on the line rattled against the walls of the house; but it lasted for only a moment; then all was quiet again, and the sun shone warmly.

The man and his wife went into their house, quickly changed from their Sunday clothes, and then hurried across the dunes, which looked like enormous waves of sand suddenly frozen in motion. The sea reed and the bluish green of the sharp dune grass alone relieved the monotony of the white sand. A couple of neighbors appeared, and all helped in pulling the boats higher up on the sandy shore, while the wind steadily strengthened and blew bitingly cold. When they returned across the dunes the waves were lifting their whitecaps; sand and sharp pebbles were beating into their faces, and the wind cut off the top ridges of some of the dunes, breaking them into sand showers.

Evening came, and a swelling sound filled the air; there was a howling and wailing like a host of despairing spirits, and even though the fisherman's hut lay near the shore, the noise of the wind drowned the roar of the sea. The sand drifted against the windowpanes, and every now and then there came a violent gust of wind that seemed to shake the house to its very foundation. It was a dark evening; the moon would not rise until nearly midnight.

The air cleared a little, but the storm was now raging with all its fury over the deep, black ocean. The fisherman and his wife had long since gone to bed, but in such weather it was impossible to close an eye.

Suddenly there was a tap at the window; the door was pushed open, and someone said, "A large ship is stranded on the outer reef!" In a moment the man and his wife were out of bed and dressing themselves hurriedly.

The Moon was up now, and it would have been light enough to see had it not been for the flying sand which forced eyes to squint. Only with great difficulty, waiting for each lull and creeping a little farther between gusts, could they make their way across the sand dunes. And now, like swansdown in the air, salty white foam flew in from the sea as it hurled its waves against the coast in boiling fury.

Only a long-experienced eye could have distinguished the ship way out there; it was a splendid two-master. At that very instant it was lifted over the reef, three or four cables' lengths off the usual channel; it drove on toward land, struck against the second reef, and there stuck fast.

It was impossible to send any help, for the sea was far too tumultuous; waves broke over the entire vessel. They imagined hearing screams of terror, the cries of death agony; they could see the aimless rushing to and fro on board; it was all hopeless, helpless. Now a wave like a thundering avalanche crashed down on the bowsprit, and then it disappeared. The stern rose high above the water, and two people could be seen leaping from it into the sea; they disappeared—a moment more—and a tremendous wave thundering toward the dunes flung a body on the shore. It was a woman, and surely she was dead! A couple of women who quickly gathered around her believed she showed signs of life, and carried her over the dunes to the fisherman's cottage. How beautiful and dainty she was!—no doubt a lady of rank.

They laid her in the fisherman's humble bed; there was no linen to wrap her in, only a woolen blanket; but at least this was warm and comfortable. She breathed, but she was in a high fever. She had no idea where she was or what had happened; perhaps this was just as well, for all that was dear to her now lay at the bottom of the ocean; they had met the same fate as those sung of in the ballad about "The King of England's Son":

A sorrowful sight it was to all;
The ship was broken into pieces small!

Many bits of the wreck were driven ashore, but the lady alone survived of all the voyagers. Still the wind howled and wailed along the coast.

For a few minutes she seemed to rest, but then came screams of pain and fear. Her beautiful eyes opened, and she spoke a few words, but no one could understand her. At last, after hours of suffering and struggles, there nestled in her arms a tiny, newborn child.

That child was to have rested under silken curtains in a beautiful home, was to have been welcomed to a life full of this world's riches; but our Lord had willed that he should be born in this humble hut; and not so much as one kiss was he to receive from the lips of his mother!

The fisherman's wife placed the baby against its mother's heart, a heart that beat no longer—she was dead. And the child who was to have been brought up in luxury and pleasure had been hurled headlong into life, tossed by the sea among the sand dunes, there to experience the lot of a poor man, and weary and dark days.

And always the old song comes to our mind:

On the king's son's cheek there was a tear
"Pray, Christ, I reach Bovbjerg; then I shan't fear!
If only I had come to Herr Bugge's Strand;
Then no knight nor squire of any band
Would have dared against me lift a hand."

The ship had been wrecked a little to the south of the Nissum Fjord, on the very shore that Herr Bugge had once called his own. The hard, cruel times of the ballad, when the dwellers on the western coast treated castaways so inhumanly, had long passed. The shipwrecked were now treated with love and kindness, as they are in our own time. The dying mother and the unfortunate child would have been treated with the utmost care and tenderness, wherever the storm had driven them; but nowhere could they have received more sincere kindness than in the hut of that poor fisherwoman who, only yesterday, had stood with a sorrowful heart beside the grave of her child who, if God had allowed him to live, would today have completed his fifth year.

No one knew the identity of the dead woman or from where she had come. The broken fragments of the wrecked ship brought no explanation.

No letter or news of the daughter and son-in-law was ever received at the rich merchant's house in Spain. They could not have reached their destination, considering the violent storms that had raged for the last few weeks. For months they waited before admitting to themselves the sad truth: "All lost! All perished!"

But in the hut of the fisherman near the sand dunes of Hunsby there was now a tiny infant.

Where God provides food for two there is sure to be enough for a third; and near the sea there is always at least a plate of fish for hungry mouths. They christened the little one Jörgen.

"Surely he must be a Jewish child," people said; "his skin is so dark." "He may just as easily be Italian or Spanish," said the clergyman. To the fisherman's wife all three races seemed very much the same, but it was a great comfort to her to know that at least the child was really a baptized Christian.

The boy thrived, his noble blood sustaining warmth and gaining strength from the poor fare as he grew in that humble hut; the Danish language, as spoken in West Jutland, became his own language. The pomegranate seed from Spain had become a sea-grass plant on Jutland's western coast, and in this home, so foreign to his inheritance, he took root for the rest of his life. He was to experience hunger and cold, a poor man's wants and troubles, but also he was to know a poor man's pleasures.

For everyone childhood has its highlights, and the memories of these sparkle throughout one's whole life. What a full share of play and pleasure he had! All the miles of shore were strewn with playthings for him; it was a mosaic of pebbles, red as coral, yellow as amber, or white and round as birds' eggs, all bright with colors and smooth and polished by the sea. Even the dried-out skeleton of a fish, the water plants, dried by the wind, or the shiny, white seaweed, long and narrow like strings fluttering among the rocks, were a delight to eye and heart. The boy was a wide-awake child, full of ability. How he could remember all the old stories or songs he had ever heard! And how clever he was with his fingers! He could make sailing ships out of stones and shells or draw pictures that were quite an ornament to the room. He could "carve his thoughts out of a stick," as his foster mother said, when he was still only a little boy, and his voice was so sweet and caught the strain of a melody so quickly! That little heart was attuned to many fine harmonies which might have rung throughout the world if he had been placed in a less narrow home than the fisherman's hut near the North Sea.

One day a box of rare flower bulbs drifted ashore after a shipwreck. Some were taken out and made into soup, with the idea that they might be good to eat; others were just left to rot in the sand and never fulfilled their destiny, never unfolded the glorious beauty of form and color that lay hidden within them. Would such be the case with Jörgen? Life was soon over for the flower bulbs, but he still had many years to live and struggle.

It never occurred either to him or his foster parents that their lives were lonely and monotonous; days went by, and there was plenty to do and hear and see. The ocean itself was a great book of lessons; every day it seemed to turn over a new page, storm or calm. A shipwreck was an exciting event. The visit to the church was a festive event. Twice a year the fisherman's hut had a visitor, and a very welcome one. This was the eel seller from Fjaltring, up near Bovbjerg, who was the brother of Jörgen's foster mother. He came with a red wagon full of eels; it was shut up like a box and had blue and white tulips painted on it. It was drawn by two black oxen, and Jörgen was permitted to drive them.

The eel man had a good head on him. He was a jolly guest; he always brought a little keg of schnapps, and everyone had a drink of it, sometimes from a coffee cup, if there were not enough glasses. Even Jörgen, little as he was, had a thimbleful; that was so he could digest the fat eels, said the eel man. Then he would tell them his old story, and whenever he heard people laugh at it, he always repeated it at once, to the very same people, as all talkative folks do. And as Jörgen used phrases from this story throughout his youth and later in life, we had better listen to it.

"The eels played out in the river, and Mother Eel said to her daughters, when they had begged for permission to explore a little way up the stream, 'Don't go too far! The wicked man with his spear will come and catch you all!' But they did go too far, and of the eight of them only three returned to their mother and wailed out their story, 'We had only gone a little distance beyond the door when the ugly man with the spear came and stabbed our five sisters to death!'

"'They'll come back,' said the eel mother.

"'No,' said the daughters. 'For he skinned them and cut them into bits and fried them.'

"'They'll surely come back,' said the eel mother.

"'Yes, but he ate them!'

"'Still they'll come back,' said the eel mother.

"'But he drank schnapps afterwards!' said the daughters.

"'Oh, my! Oh my!' howled the eel mother. 'Then they'll never return! For schnapps drowns eels!'

"And for that very reason people should always take a little schnapps after eating them," finished the eel spearer.

And this story ran like a thread of gold tinsel—his most humorous recollection—through the web of Jörgen's life. He too wanted to go past the threshold, "a little way up the river," or rather out into the wide world in a ship; but his foster mother objected, just as Mother Eel had objected, "There are so many wicked men with spears." He longed to go a little past the sand dunes into the heath. And at last he did for four pleasant days, the brightest of his whole childhood; and he saw all of Jutland's happy, homelike beauty and sunshine. He went to a party; it was a funeral party.

A wealthy relative of the fisherman had died; his farm was far inland, "to the east, a bit northerly," as the saying goes. Jörgen's foster parents had to go, and they took him with them. They passed from the dunes over heath and swamp to the green pastures where the Skjaerum River hollows out its bed—that brook full of eels, where lived Mother Eel and her daughters whom the wicked people speared and cut in pieces. And hadn't men often acted just as cruelly toward their fellow men? The good knight, Sir Bugge, whose name lives in the old song, was murdered by wicked men; and, though he himself was called "good," he is said to have come very close to slaying the architect who built his castle, with its tower and thick walls, on the slope where the brook Skjaerum falls into the Nissum Fjord, just where Jörgen now stood with his foster parents. The ramparts and the red crumbling fragments of the walls could still be seen.

It was here that Sir Bugge, after the architect had left, ordered one of his men to follow him. "Say to him, 'Master, the tower leans to one side.' And if he turns and looks to find out, you must slay him and take from him the money I have paid him; but if he turns not, let him depart in peace." The man obeyed, but the architect did not turn; rather did he answer clearly and boldly. "The tower does not lean, for I have built it well; but one day a man shall come from the west in a blue cloak, and he shall make it lean." And a hundred years later this came to pass, for the North Sea broke in and the tower collapsed; but Predbjörn Gyldenstjerne, who owned the castle at that time, built a new mansion on the slope higher up; this is still standing, and is called Nörre Vosborg.

Jörgen and his foster parents had to pass this place, so now he saw this and other spots that he had heard stories about in the long winter evenings. He saw the castle, with its double moats choked with trees and bushes and its rampart overhung with bracken. But the loveliest sight to him were the tall lime trees that reached right up to the roof and filled the air with fragrance. In the northwest corner of the garden stood a large bush bearing flowers as white as snow—they seemed strange to him among the green leaves of summer. It was an elder bush, the first he had seen blooming; that bush and the lime trees were stored safely away throughout the years in a corner of his mind, a bit of the fragrance and beauty of Denmark, "kept to delight the old man."

The journey continued and became still more pleasant, for outside Nörre Vosborg, where they had found the flowering elder bush, they met other people who were also going to the funeral, and drove on with them. Of course, all three of them had to sit on a little wooden chest with iron trimmings at the rear of the carriage, but they decided even that was better than walking. The carriage rolled away over the rough hillocks of the heath, and the oxen that drew it stopped to graze whenever a patch of fresh grass appeared among the heather. The sun shone warmly, and they saw the strange sight of rising smoke in the distance, as transparent as though beams of light were rolling and dancing over the heath. "That is Loki driving his flock," people said, and that was enough explanation for Jörgen. He felt as though he were driving right into fairyland—and yet everything was real! And how still it all was about them!

The heath spread out before them, a wide, rich carpet, with the heather in blossom. Mingled with the dark green juniper and fresh oak shoots, it studded the ground as if with bouquets. This was an inviting place to throw oneself down, if it were not for the many poisonous snakes people said were there. And people spoke too of the wolves that used to be found there so often that the district was known as Ulvborg Herred. The old man who was driving the wagon told them how, in his father's day, the horses often had fierce battles with wild beasts since exterminated, and how one morning he found a horse trampling on a wolf he had slain, while his own legs were quite bare of flesh which had been gnawed off in the struggle.

The wagon rolled too quickly over the rough heath and through the deep sand. They reached the house of mourning, where they found many strangers inside and outside; many wagons stood side by side, with their horses or oxen turned out to seek meager pasture; from the back of the house great sand dunes, like those at home near the sea, extended far and wide. How could they be here? It was twelve miles into the country, yet they were as tall and large as those by the shore. The wind had lifted them up and blown them here; they too had a history.

Psalms were sung, and a few of the older people wept, but aside from this, everything was very pleasant, Jörgen thought. There was plenty to eat and drink; the finest fat eels, with schnapps afterwards "to settle the eels," as the eel seller had said. And his words were certainly carried out at this gathering.

Jörgen went in and out of the house, and by the third day he was as thoroughly at home there as in the fisherman's hut among his own sand dunes, where he had spent all his life. But the heath here was far more beautiful, with its myriads of brilliant blossoms and luscious sweet bilberries, growing so thickly that if one stepped on them, the ground became stained with their red juice. Here lay an old Viking grave, and near it lay another. When the mysterious columns of mist curled upward through the calm air, they said, "The heath is on fire." It shone brightest toward evening.

But the fourth day came at last and brought the end of the wake; it was time to return from the inland sand dunes to the coastal sand dunes.

"Ours are the real ones after all," said the father. "These have no strength."

Then they talked about the sand dunes and how they came to be here, and this was very interesting. The peasants found a corpse on the shore and buried it in the churchyard; then the sand began to fly about, and the sea broke in with violence. A wise man of the parish advised that the grave be opened, for if the stranger were found sucking his thumb, they could then be sure that he whom they had buried was a merman and that the sea would not rest till it had fetched him back. So they opened the grave, and sure enough, the dead man lay with his thumb between his lips. He was quickly laid on a cart drawn by two oxen, and as though stung by hornets they rushed with him over heath and moor to the sea. That stopped the shower of flying sand, but the dunes that it formed are still there.

That was what Jörgen learned and carried away with him from the happiest days of his childhood—those four days at the funeral party.

How wonderful it was, he thought, to go out into the world and see new places and new people! And he was to go still farther away. Before he had finished his fourteenth year—he was still a child—he did actually go out to look at he world, through the eyes of a cabin boy. Now he had to endure bad weather, rough seas, and evil men; scanty fare, cold nights, the rope's end, and blows from a hard fist—yes, such were his experiences. There was something in his noble Spanish blood that continually boiled over and brought hot words to his lips. He soon learned it was wisest to restrain them, but in doing so, he felt somewhat as the eel must feel when it is skinned, cut up, and tossed into the frying pan. "I shall return again!" said a voice within him.

Now the ship touched at the Spanish coast, the home of Jörgen's parents, in fact at the very town where they used to live in splendor and happiness. But he knew nothing of his homeland or his relatives, and even less did his family know of him. The shabby cabin boy was not even permitted to go ashore while the others went; but on the last day it happened that some provisions had been bought, and Jörgen was told to carry them on board.

There stood Jörgen in his wretched clothes that looked as if they had been washed in a ditch and dried in a chimney; this was the first time that he, the dweller of the sand dunes, had ever seen a great city. How tall the houses were, how narrow the streets, swarming with human beings constantly rushing to and fro, a regular whirlpool of townspeople and farmers, monks and soldiers—a clamor, a screaming, a jangling of bells from asses and mules, a clanging of bigger bells from the churches—song and musical instruments—knocking and hammering, for every tradesman seemed to have his shop either on his threshold or on the sidewalk. And all the while the hot sun burned down, and the air was heavy. It was as if one had entered a bake oven full of beetles, cockchafers, bees, and flies, all humming and buzzing with all their might; Jörgen hardly knew if he were walking or standing still.

Suddenly he saw before him the mighty portals of a cathedral, with lights streaming out through the twilight of the colonnades and the fragrance of incense saluting him. Even the poorest beggar in rags could venture to climb those stairs and enter. The sailor who had taken Jörgen ashore went into the church; Jörgen followed, and soon he stood in the sanctuary. Colored pictures glowed out from golden backgrounds; amid flowers and candles at the altar he beheld the Blessed Virgin holding the Holy Child; priests in their vestments were chanting, while pretty choirboys swung silver censers. What magnificence he saw there! All this glory and beauty, streaming into Jörgen's soul, nearly overpowered him. The church and the faith of his fathers surrounded him and awakened a chord in his soul, causing tears to come to his eyes.

From the cathedral they proceeded to the market. A heavy load of provisions was piled upon him. It was a long way back, and when he grew tired he wanted to rest in front of a large and splendid palace decorated with statues and marble pillars, with broad steps. But as he rested his burden against the wall a porter dressed in gold lace bustled out, waving a silver-headed cane, and drove him away—him, the grandson of that house! But no one knew it, himself least of all.

And so he returned to the ship and accepted, as before, his share of cuffs, broken slumbers, and hard work. Such was his first experience in life! "It is good for a man to bear the yoke in his youth," they say: "Yes, if he makes up for it in old age."

When the term of his signing on was ended and the ship was anchored in the Ringkjöbing Fjord, he went home to the Hunsby sand dunes. But his foster mother was dead—she had died during his voyage.

A hard winter followed, with snowstorms raging over sea and land. It was difficult to get from one place to another. How differently are things divided in this life. Here were icy cold and driving snowstorms, while in Spain the sun burned too fiercely. And yet one clear frosty day, while Jörgen watched the swans flying from the ocean across the Nissum Fjord toward Nörre Vosborg, he felt that here, in the northern land, he could breathe more freely. And Denmark had its beauty of summer too; he imagined he could see the heath with its flowers and ripe, juicy berries, while the lime trees and elder bush of Nörre Vosborg stood blooming before him. He must go back there again.

It was toward spring, and the fishing began. Jörgen helped, for he had grown during the last year; he was quick and alert at his work, and there was no lack of spirit in him. He could swim and tread water, turn over and tumble in the water. They often warned him to beware of the mackerel shoals, which, it is said, seize the best swimmer, drag him down into the water, and eat him—that would be the end of him. But that never happened to Jörgen.

Among his neighbors on the sand dunes was boy named Morten. He and Jörgen had become good friends, and now they shipped out together on a vessel bound for Norway. Afterwards, they went to Holland together. They had never quarreled, but when one is hot-blooded by nature, one can easily start something; and that Jörgen did one day, over nothing.

They were sitting together, behind the cabin door, eating off the same clay dish, when Jörgen, who held his pocket knife in his hand, raised it toward Morten with a threatening gesture, his cheeks deadly pale and his eyes blazing with fury. But Morten only said, "So you're the sort who uses a knife!" At those words Jörgen's hand was lowered; he said no word, but finished his dinner and went off to work Morten and said, "Hit me in the face! I deserve it. There's something in me that's always boiling over."

"Oh, forget it," said Morten, and they became better friends than ever.

When they had returned home to the sand dunes and people heard the story of this quarrel, they said that Jörgen was like a pot that easily boiled over, but that he was an honest pot, anyway.

"But he's no Jutlander. No one can call him a Jutland pot," was Morten's witty answer.

They were both young and healthy, well built, and with strong limbs. Jörgen was the more active.

Up in Norway the peasants go into the mountains and take their cattle there to find pasture. On the western coast of Jutland, the fisherman build huts among the sand dunes. They build them with planks from shipwrecks and cover them over with heath and turf; here the fishermen live and sleep during the early spring. Each fisherman has a girl as a servant—she is called his aesepige; she supplies the bait for the hooks, must be ready on the wharf with warm ale to refresh him, and cooks his food when he returns to his hut, tired and hungry. The girls carry the fish up from the boat, cut it up, and, in short, have plenty to do.

Jörgen, his foster father, a few other fishermen, and their girls had a hut together; Morten lived in the next hut.

One of the girls, named Elsa, had known Jörgen ever since they were both little children; they were quite fond of each other and always happy to be together. They were much alike in disposition, but quite different in appearance, for Jörgen was very dark-complexioned, while her skin was white, her hair as yellow as flax, and her eyes as blue as the sea on a sunny day.

One day Elsa and Jörgen were walking together, and Jörgen was holding her hand in a warm, fervent grasp, when she said to him, "Jörgen, I want to unburden my heart to you. Let me be your aesepige, instead of Morten's. I know he has hired me, but you're like a brother to me, and Morten—he and I are sweethearts. But now, don't go and tell everybody else about it!"

Jörgen felt as if the sand dunes were whirling beneath him. He didn't say a word; he only nodded—and that was the same as saying, "Yes." This was all that was necessary to make him feel a bitter hatred in his heart for Morten. The more he thought about it, the clearer he realized that Morten had robbed him of the only creature he loved. Never before had he understood his own feelings toward Elsa, and now all hope of winning her for himself was gone.

When the fishermen are returning home over a fairly rough sea, it is interesting to see how the boats pass over the sand reefs. One man stands upright while the rest watch him, sitting with their oars ready to use the moment he signals that a great wave is coming which will lift the boat over the reef. It comes, and the vessel is tossed up so that its very keel can be seen from the shore; in another moment the entire boat vanishes from sight and neither boat, men, nor mast can be seen—you might imagine the ocean has swallowed everything up; another moment, and the boat reappears, crawling up the wave like a mighty sea monster, its oars moving like the creature's legs. The second and third reefs are crossed in the same way, and then the fisherman spring into shallow water and drag their boat ashore. Every wave helps them, until finally they have it beyond the reach of the breakers. But the slightest mistake in the signal when passing those reefs, the delay of a moment, and they would be shipwrecked.

"It would soon be all over with me and Morten too, if that happened," came into Jörgen's mind out at sea. They were approaching the outer reef when his foster father suddenly became seriously ill; the fever had seized him. Jörgen jumped up and stood in the bow. "Father, let me take your place!" he said; and his eyes moved from Morten to the sea, and from the sea back to Morten, as the oars swung on with the steady strokes, and the great wave rolled toward them. Then suddenly his look fell on the pale face of his foster father, and he could not obey his wicked impulse. The boat crossed the reefs in safety, and in safety they came ashore. But that evil thought still lurked in Jörgen's heart and roused every little fiber of bitterness that he remembered from his childhood days; but he could not weave the fibers together, so he dismissed it all from his mind.

He felt that Morten had robbed him, and that was reason enough to hate him. Some of the fishermen noticed the change in Jörgen, but Morten himself saw nothing; he was just the same as ever, ready to help and eager to talk—in fact, a little too much of the latter.

Jörgen's foster father took to his bed; it became his death bed, for a week later he was dead. Jörgen was his heir, now master of the cottage behind the sand dunes. It was a poor enough hut, but still it was something; and Morten didn't have so much.

"I suppose you won't go to sea again, Jörgen," said one of the old fishermen. "You'll always stay with us now."

But that was by no means Jörgen's thought; on the contrary, he thought about seeing some more of the world. The eel seller up at Fjaltring had a cousin up at Old Skagen, also a fisherman, but wealthy, and a shipowner too; they said he was a kindly old man with whom it would be very pleasant to take service. Old Skagen lies way up at the northern part of Jutland, as far away from the Hunsby sand dunes as one can go; that part of the idea pleased Jörgen best; he had no intention of attending the wedding of Elsa and Morten, which was to take place in a couple of weeks.

It was foolish for Jörgen to go away, said the old fisherman; now that he had a house of his own Elsa would very likely prefer him to Morten. Jörgen's reply was so abrupt that it wasn't easy to make out his meaning. The old man brought Elsa to him; she didn't say much, but she did say: "You have a house; that must be considered."

And Jörgen did consider many things. The ocean has its heavy waves, but the waves of the human heart are even heavier; many thoughts, strong and weak, passed through Jörgen's heart and head before he asked Elsa, "Suppose Morten had a house as good as mine; which of us would you rather have?"

"But Morten doesn't have one, and never will have one."

"But suppose he did have one."

"Why then I'd take Morten, of course; for that's the way I feel about him! But one must have something to live on."

All night Jörgen thought over this answer. There was something within him, he found, something he himself couldn't figure out; it was stronger even than his love for Elsa.

He went to Morten, and what he said and did had been well considered; he offered to sell his house to him on the lowest possible terms, explaining that it would please him better to go to sea again. When Elsa heard about it, she thanked him with a kiss, for she really did love Morten better.

Jörgen was going to leave early next morning. Late the evening before, he had a sudden desire to go to see Morten once more. On his way among the sand dunes he met the old fisherman, who greatly disapproved of his leaving and who declared Morten must carry a charm sewn up in his pocket to make the young girls fall in love with him. Jörgen brushed aside such talk and bade him farewell. Then he proceeded to Morten's hut where he heard loud voices; evidently Morten was not alone. For a moment Jörgen stood irresolute; least of all did he want to meet Elsa there, and now that he thought it over, he would prefer not having Morten thank him all over again. So he turned back without entering.

Next morning, before daylight, he tied up his bundle, gathered his provisions, and started through the sand dunes to the shore. It was easier walking by the sea than along the heavy, sandy road, and besides it was shorter, for he was going first to Fjaltring, near Bovbjerg, where lived the eel seller, whom he had promised to visit.

The ocean was smooth and blue, and as he walked he crushed under his feet the shells and pebbles, the playthings of his childhood. As he was walking his nose began to bleed, and a couple of large drops fell on his sleeve; it seemed a trivial enough matter, but a trivial matter can sometimes be of importance. He soon stopped the bleeding, wiped his sleeve, and walked on. It seemed as if this had cleared both his heart and head. When he found sea kale growing in the sand, he broke off a branch and stuck it in his hat, determined to be joyful and happy; wasn't he going out into the world "a little way up the river," as the young eels had so longed to do? "But beware of wicked people, who will spear you, skin you, cut you in pieces, and lay you in dishes!" he repeated to himself. "I'll slip through the world whole-skinned. Courage is a strong weapon."

The sun was already high when he reached the narrow inlet between the North Sea and the Nissum Fjord; then he looked back and made out in the distance two men on horseback with others following them, all riding at great speed. This did not concern him.

The ferryboat was on the opposite side of the bay, but Jörgen shouted till it came across for him. He sprang on board, but before the ferry was halfway across, the men who had followed him on horseback arrived on the shore, and with threatening gestures called for him to return in the name of the law. Jörgen couldn't imagine what it meant, but thought it would be best to return; so he took the oar himself, and rowed back. In an instant the men had leaped into the boat and before he was aware of it, they had bound his hands together with a rope. "It's well you're caught!" they said. "Your crime will cost you your life!"

He was accused of nothing less than murder! Morten had been found stabbed in the neck with a knife; late, the evening before, one of the fishermen had met Jörgen on his way to Morten's house, and it was remembered that it wasn't the first time Jörgen had threatened Morten with a knife; there seemed no doubt that he was the murderer.

Now the question was where to confine him. Ringkjöbing was the proper place, but it was a long way off, and the wind was against them. In less than half an hour they had crossed Skjaerum Fjord, and now they were only a quarter of a mile from Nörre Vosborg, which was a strong mansion with moats and ramparts. One of the men in the boat was the brother of the keeper of this mansion; he suggested that they might get permission to confine Jörgen, for the time being, in the dungeon where Long Margrethe, the gypsy, had been imprisoned until her execution.

No one listened to Jörgen's denials, and those few drops of blood on his shirt were silent witnesses against him. Conscious of his innocence and of the fact that there was no chance of his being cleared, he calmly resigned himself to his fate.

They landed near the old rampart, where the castle of Sir Bugge had stood—it was the very same spot that Jörgen's feet had trodden years before when he had gone with his foster parents to the funeral party, where he had spent those four happy days on the heath. By the very same path they now led him up to Nörre Vosborg; and here, as then, the elder bush was in full bloom, and the tall lime trees wafted their fragrance to him—he might have imagined it was only yesterday that he had been here last.

Under the grand staircase in the western wing of the building a passage leads into a low-roofed vaulted cell; it was from here that Long Margrethe was led to her execution. She had confessed to having devoured the hearts of five children and believed that, could she have eaten two more, she would have been able to make herself invisible and fly away. In the cell was a tiny, narrow airhole in the wall; but the lime trees outside sent none of their refreshing fragrance within; all was cold, damp, and moldy. There was only a rough bench in the cell; but a good conscience makes an easy pillow, so Jörgen could really lie comfortably.

The thick wooden door was closed and the iron bolts were shot, but superstition can creep through the keyhole of a mansion as well as a fisherman's hut; and as Jörgen lay in the silence and darkness he could not help thinking of Long Margrethe and her horrible crimes. Her last thoughts had filled that narrow dungeon the night before her execution. Nor could he help remembering the black arts that had been practiced by the owner of this mansion, Herr Swanwedel, when he lived there many years ago, and how the watchdog that guarded the bridge had every morning been found hung in his chains across the railing. Such thoughts came to Jörgen's mind and made him shiver; but a sunbeam, a refreshing thought from without, also came to his mind, the remembrance of the blossoming elder and lime trees.

He was not left here long, but was removed to Ringkjöbing; but there his imprisonment was none the less rigorous. For Jörgen's times were not like ours; they were hard times for poor men; peasant farms and peasant settlements were still being converted into new knights' estates. The coachman or valet of a nobleman was often appointed village judge, with power to condemn the peasant to a severe flogging or the loss of all his property for some trifling offense. And thus, in Jutland, far from "The King's Copenhagen" and the wise and just rulers of state, the law took its course with little regard for justice. Jörgen could expect that his case would be delayed.

His wretched cell was bitterly cold; when would this misery end? Innocent, he had been thrown into misfortune and sorrow; that was his lot! He had plenty of time to think over the hard dealing that this world had given him and to wonder why this fate had been allotted him. Still, all would correct itself in that "second life" which assuredly awaits us. In the poor fisherman's cottage that faith had taken firm root in his soul; the light that, even amid the sunshine and plenty of Spain, could not pierce the darkness of his father's mind was sent to him to comfort him in poverty and distress, a sign of the mercy of God, which never disappoints.

Now the spring storms settled in. The roaring of the North Sea can be heard for miles inland, and when the tempests abate there is a thundering as of hundreds of heavy wagons rolling over a hard tunneled road. In his dungeon Jörgen heard this sound, and it was a relief to him; no old melodies could so move him as the music of the rolling ocean—the boundless ocean that had carried him throughout the world with the speed of winds—the ocean over which men pass, carrying their own house with them like the snails carry theirs, always standing on their own native ground, even in foreign lands. How he listened to that deep thunder! How his thoughts surged into a turmoil within him! Free, free! How wonderful to be free—even if with a patched shirt and shoes without soles! Sometimes his soul burned with indignant anger, and he pounded the wall with his clenched fist.

Weeks, months, a whole year passed, and then the gypsy

Niels Tyv, the horse dealer, as he was called, was picked up, and then better times came; it was established that Jörgen was innocent.

The evening before Jörgen's departure—the night of the murder—Morten and Niels Tyv had met at a little tavern north of Ringkjöbing Fjord. A couple of glasses were emptied, not enough to get drunk on, but enough to loosen Morten's tongue; he began to boast of having bought a house and of getting married, and when Niels asked from where he was getting the money, Morten proudly slapped his hand to his pocket.

"The money's here, right where it ought to be," he said. This boast cost him his life, for when he rose to go Niels followed him and stabbed him in the back with a knife—all for the sake of money that was not in his pocket at all.

There was a great deal of talk about the affair, but for us it is enough to know that Jörgen was released. But what compensation did he receive for the long, weary days he spent in the cold and loneliness, and for being despised by his fellowman? Why, he was told it was lucky for him he was innocent; now he could go. To be sure, the mayor gave him ten marks for traveling expenses, and several citizens of Ringkjöbing offered him beer and good food, for there are a few kind hearts in the world; not all men "spear, skin, and devour" their fellows.

But the best thing of all was that a merchant from Skagen named Brönne—the same man with whom Jörgen had intended to take service before his imprisonment—had come to Ringkjöbing on business at just that time and heard the whole story. He was kindhearted and sympathized with Jörgen's sufferings; now he would do him a little kindness and prove to him that there are some good people in the world.

Out of prison, not only to freedom, but to a paradise of love and kindness! But it is no man's fate to drain a cup of unmixed bitterness. If even man could not endure to offer such to his fellow man, how could the all-loving God?

"Let the past be dead and buried," said Merchant Brönne. "We'll draw a heavy black line over the last year and burn the calendar, and in two days we'll be off together for Skagen—happy, friendly, peaceful Skagen! People call it the out-of-the-way corner of the country; it's a blessed chimney corner, with windows opening out to the whole wide world!"

What a journey! To breathe the fresh air again; to emerge from the cold damp prison air into the warm sunshine! The heath was gay with blooming heather; the shepherd boy perched on a warrior's grave mound, shrilling his flute made from sheep bones; Fata Morgana, the beautiful mirage of the desert, flaunted her hanging gardens and floating woods; and the wonderful transparent phenomenon called "Loki driving his flock" could be seen.

They traveled up toward the Lime Fjord, toward Skagen, through the land of the Vends, whence the men with the long beards—which had earned them the name of Lombards—had emigrated when, in the days of the famine under King Snio, it was decreed that all the children and old people should be put to death. But Gambaruk, a noble woman of great wealth, had proposed instead that all the young should leave the country.

Jörgen was learned enough to know all this, and although he had never seen the land of the Lombards beyond the Alps, he could easily picture it to himself, for had he not in his boyhood seen the south, Spain? He could remember clearly the piled heaps of fruit, the scarlet pomegranate blossoms, the noise and din and ringing of bells in that great beehive of a city. But he still loved best the land of his home, and Jörgen's home was Denmark.

At last they reached "Vendilskaga," as Skagen is called in the old Norse and Icelandic sagas. Even then old Skagen, with its Easter and Westertown, stretched for miles with sand dunes and farmland as far as the lighthouse near Grenen. Houses and farms were strewn among the shifting sand dunes—it is a wild land where the wind plays constantly in the loose sand, and where the screams of sea gulls, sea swallows, and wild swans cut sharply through the eardrum.

A few miles southwest of Grenen is High or Old Skagen; here Merchant Brönne lived, and here Jörgen would now live. The house was tarred; each of the little outhouses had an inverted boat for a roof, and driftwood joined together formed the pigsty. There was no enclosure, for there was nothing to enclose; but on ropes, strung in long rows one above another, hung countless fishes drying in the wind. The whole shore was strewn with dead herring; in fact, the nets could hardly be thrown into the sea before they would be filled with them. Great loads of herring were caught and taken inland. They were so plentiful that many were often thrown back into the sea or left to rot on the sand.

The merchant's wife and daughter, and even the servants, rushed out in delight to greet the father when they arrived home. There was such handshaking, so much noise, so much to talk about! And the daughter had such a sweet face and lovely eyes!

The house was cozy and roomy inside; the table was set

with plates of fish, flounder fit for a king, and wine from Skagen's own vineyard, the great ocean, from which the grapes drifted ashore already pressed, both in barrels and bottles.

When mother and daughter had heard who Jörgen was, and learned how cruelly he, an innocent man, had been treated, they looked upon him with kindness, and the beautiful Miss Clara's bright eyes sparkled more warmly than before.

Jörgen found a blessed home in Old Skagen; it did his heart good; it had suffered so much cruelty, even the bitterness of love, which either softens or hardens the heart. But Jörgen was still young, his heart still soft, and there was a vacant place in it. For that reason it was perhaps just as well that in three weeks Clara was to sail for Christiansand, in Norway, to spend the winter with an aunt.

The Sunday before her departure, all were to go together to Holy Communion. The church was large and stately, built by the Dutch and Scotch many centuries before, and quite a distance from where the town is now situated. The church was somewhat dilapidated now, and the way through the deep sand made hard walking, but people did not mind these difficulties to get to the house of God to sing psalms, and to hear the sermon. The sand was piled up outside the wall around the cemetery, but the graves had still been kept free of it.

It was the largest church north of the Lime Fjord. The Virgin Mary, with a golden crown on her head and the infant Savior in her arms, was painted in bright colors above the altar; the holy apostles were ranged around the choir, and high on the wall there hung portraits of Skagen's old burgomasters and councilmen, with their insignia of office. The pulpit was carved. The sun shone brightly into the church, lighting up the polished brass chandelier and the little vessel that hung down from the roof. Jörgen was overwhelmed by the same pure, childlike feeling of devotion that had thrilled his soul when, a boy, he had stood in the rich Spanish cathedral. But here the feeling was different, for in this place he felt that he was one of the congregation.

After the sermon came the communion, and when Jörgen knelt with the others to receive the consecrated bread and wine, he found that he was kneeling next to Miss Clara. But his thoughts were so raised to God and the holy sacrament that not until they rose did he realize that she had been his neighbor. Then he saw the salt tears rolling down her cheeks.

Two days later she sailed for Norway, and Jörgen went out to help on the farm and with the fishing; there were more fish to be caught there in those days than there are now. Shoals of mackerel shone brightly in the darkness of the night, thus betraying the course they were following. The sea robins snarled, and the crabs gave pitiful cries when they were caught; fish are not as voiceless as people say. Jörgen was more quiet than they; he kept his secret—and yet someday it would perhaps burst forth.

Every Sunday when he sat in church and his eyes rested on the picture of the Virgin Mother, they also paused a moment on the spot where Miss Clara had knelt beside him, and he thought of her and her kindness to him.

The autumn brought its rain and sleet. The water rose up in the town of Skagen, for the sand could not absorb it all; people had to wade through it, and sometimes even sail through the streets in boats. Snowstorms and sandstorms followed; ship after ship was wrecked on those fatal reefs; the sand whirled about and buried the houses until the occupants had to creep out through the chimneys. But that was not an unusual occurrence there. Indoors were comfort and warmth; the blazing and crackling fires were fed with peat or with dried wood from the wrecks, and Merchant Brönne read aloud from an old chronicle. He read about Prince Hamlet of Denmark and of how he landed from England and fought a great battle near Bovbjerg; his grave was at Ramme, only a few miles from the eel seller's home, where the heath was like an immense cemetery, studded with hundreds of Viking grave mounds. Merchant Brönne had visited Hamlet's grave. There was more talk of the olden days and of their English and Scottish neighbors, and then Jörgen sang the old ballad about "The King of England's Son," about the stately ship, and how it was decked out:

The blessed words of our dear Lord
Were written in gold on panels aboard.
On the prow, in colors rare,
The king's son clasped his maiden fair.

Jörgen sang this verse with especial sincerity, while his eyes, luminous and black from his birth, sparkled with more fire than ever.

Thus the evenings passed pleasantly, with song and reading; all were happy in that house, even the very animals. The tin shelves gleamed with clean plates; hams and sausages hung under the ceiling and they had winter supplies in abundance. Many rich farmhouses like this are still to be found in West Jutland, abundant as this one in good comfort, good cheer, good sense, and good humor, and like the tent of an Arab for hospitality.

Jörgen had never spent so happy a time, at least since

the four days of the funeral, when he was a child. And still Miss Clara was absent; but she was never absent from their thoughts or conversation. In April a vessel was to be sent out to Norway to bring her home, and Jörgen was to go with it.

He had become so joyous and hearty, Mother Brönne said that it was a pleasure to look at him.

"And so it is to look at you!" said the old merchant. "Jörgen has put new life in our winter evenings, and in Mother, too. Why, you have grown younger this year! You were once the prettiest girl in Viborg, and that's saying a lot, for I've always considered the girls of Viborg to be the prettiest."

Jörgen said nothing in reply, but he couldn't help thinking of one Skagen girl, the one he was to bring home.

One morning Merchant Brönne went out to the lighthouse, which stands quite some distance from old Skagen, but not far from Grenen. The signal lights had been extinguished for quite some time, for the sun was already high when he climbed the tower. Four miles from the extreme point of land the sand reefs stretched under water. Many ships could be seen that day, and among them, with the help of his telescope, he believed he could distinguish the Karen Brönne; that was the name of his vessel. Yes, there she was, sailing home with Clara and Jörgen on board! Clara sat on the deck and saw the sand dunes slowly appear in the distance. If the wind held, they would be home in an hour. So near were they to home and its happiness, so near to death and its terrors.

Suddenly a plank gave way in the ship, and the water poured in! They tried to plug the leak; the pumps worked furiously; the sails came down, and the distress flag was hoisted. They were still four miles out at sea, and the fishing boats that they could see were too far off. The wind carried them landward; the tide was in their favor; but they were not strong enough. When the ship began to sink, Jörgen threw his right arm about Clara.

What a look she gave him as, crying on the holy name of our Lord, he leaped with her into the ocean! She shrieked in terror, but she knew he would never let go his hold.

On the prow, in colors rare,
The king's son clasped his maiden fair.

Jörgen acted out the old words in this moment of terror and peril; how fortunate that he was an excellent swimmer! He made his way with his feet and one free hand, the other clasped tightly around the girl. Now he floated; now he trod water with his feet, using every trick he knew to husband his strength so that it might last till he reached shore. When he heard the girl sigh, and felt a shuddering thrill pass through her body, he only held her closer. Now a wave rolled over them, but the current still carried them on; the water was so deep and clear that for a moment he fancied he saw shoals of mackerel flashing beneath them—or was it Leviathan, waiting to devour them? Shadows of the clouds swept over the water, to be followed by dazzling sunshine; flocks of birds flew screaming overhead while wild ducks, heavily and sleepily drifting on the surface of the water, started into the air in panic at the sight of the swimmer. Jörgen felt his strength going fast when he was only a few cables' lengths from shore. But help was coming—a boat was drawing near! Just then he distinctly saw a white figure in the water. A wave lifted him up; the figure came nearer; he felt a stunning shock, and everything became dark around him.

There on the sand reef lay the wreck of a ship with the sea

partly covering it; the white figurehead leaned against an anchor, and only the sharp iron edge projected above the water. Driven on by the fatal force of the current, Jörgen had struck against this figurehead; in a daze he sank with his burden, but the next wave lifted him and the young girl.

The fisherman got them both into his boat; blood was streaming over Jörgen's face, and he looked as if he were dead; but he still held the girl so tightly they had to tear her from his arm. They placed Clara, pale and lifeless, in the boat and rowed toward Grenen. All methods of restoring her were tried, but in vain—she was dead. For some time Jörgen must have been carrying a corpse, struggling and wrestling for the life of one who was already dead.

Jörgen still breathed, and they carried him to the nearest cottage in the sand dunes. A sort of army surgeon—he was also a smith and a trader—who happened to be on the spot bound up his wound, and the next day a physician was sent for from Hjörring.

But his brain was affected; he lay raving and uttering wild cries until the third day, when he fell into a sort of trance. It seemed his life hung by a thread, and for this thread to give way, the doctor said, was the best wish they could have for him. "Let us pray for our Lord to take him; he will never be a man again."

But life did not leave him; the thread did not break, though memory and all other faculties of the mind were injured. It was horrible! Only a living body was left, a body that soon regained health and strength.

Jörgen remained in Merchant Brönne's home. "He lost his mind trying to save our child," said the old man. "He is now our son!"

"Crazy": that was what they called Jörgen now, but it was hardly the right word; he was like a musical instrument with loosened strings that have lost the power of sound. Very rarely, and only for a few moments, would the old power seem to return; then they would give old melodies, or a few chords would be played. Sometimes pictures of the past would seem to rise before his mind, but then they would fade away into the mist, and once more he would sit with a blank, motionless, thoughtless face. We can only hope that he did not suffer. His dark eyes had lost their brightness and looked like black clouded glass.

"Poor crazy Jörgen," people said. And this was he who before he was born, was destined to have such a rich, earthly fortune and such happiness that it would be arrogance, terrible vanity, even to wish for or believe in an afterlife. Were all the fine qualities of his soul wasted? Only cruel days, anguish, and broken hopes had been his lot. He was like a precious root which is torn from its rich soil and flung out to rot in the sand. Could this really be the destiny of a soul created in the image of God—a mere game, battered by the chances of this world? No! The God of love will compensate him in another life for all that he lost and suffered in this. "The Lord is loving unto every man, and his mercy is over all His works." The pious old wife of Merchant Brönne repeated these words from the Psalms of David in faith and comfort, and she prayed that our Lord would soon end Jörgen's life of sorrow and take him to enjoy "God's gift of grace," the life everlasting.

Clara lay buried in the churchyard, where the sand drifted over the walls, but Jörgen did not seem to know this. It never penetrated the narrow world of his thoughts, which lived only in fragments from the past. Every Sunday he accompanied the family to church, and sat quietly with a blank face. Once, during the psalm singing, he sighed deeply, and his eyes took on life. He was gazing at the altar, at the very spot where, over a year ago, he had knelt beside his dead friend; his face turned white, his lips murmured her name, and the tears rolled down his cheeks.

They gently led him from the church, but he told them that he was well, and that he had no recollection of what had happened. Poor soul, tried indeed, but not rejected by our Lord! For who dares doubt that God, our Creator, is all-wise and all-loving? Our hearts and our minds give us this truth, and the Bible confirms it. "His mercy is over all His works."

In Spain, where gilded Moorish cupolas are fanned by the warm breezes amid laurels and orange trees, and where song and castanets are heard, a childless old man, the rich merchant, sat in his beautiful palace, sadly watching a procession of pretty children passing through the street with torches and waving banners. How much of his wealth would he not give to have such children himself! He thought of his daughter and her child who perhaps had never seen the light of this world, hence would never attain the glory of Paradise. "Poor child!"

Yes, "Poor child!" indeed—a child still, though past thirty years old; for Jörgen had lived thus for many years in Old Skagen.

The flying sand had drifted over the graves in the churchyard up to the very walls of the church; here among those who had gone before them, among relatives and friends, the dead were still being buried. Merchant Brönne and his wife now rested here under the white sand, among their children.

It was early in the year, the time of storms; the sand curled up like smoke from the sand dunes; the ocean tossed huge waves; large flocks of birds, like storm clouds, flew screaming overhead; and ship after ship was wrecked on those fatal reefs that stretched along the coast from Skagen to the Hunsby sand dunes.

One afternoon, as Jörgen sat alone in his room, a sudden light broke in his mind; it was the same restless feeling that had often in his younger years driven him out over the sand dunes or the heath.

"Home! Home!" he said. No one heard him. He left the house, and sand and pebbles whirled around him and beat into his face. He went toward the church, where the sand lay drifted up against the wall and half covered the windows. The church door was unlocked and easy to open; Jörgen went in.

The wind raged and howled over the town of Skagen; such a hurricane had not been known within the memory of man. It was awful weather! But Jörgen was sheltered within the house of God, and while black night reigned outside, within him everything grew bright—bright with the light of the immortal soul. He felt as if the heavy stone in his head had burst with a clang! He imagined that the organ was playing, but it was only the storm and the roaring of the ocean that he heard. As he sat down in one of the pews he thought the candles were being lighted, one by one, until there was a blaze of light such as he had only seen in the land of the Spaniards. Then all the portraits of the old councillors and burgomasters came to life; they stepped down from the walls where they had hung for so many years and seated themselves in the choir. Then the gates and doors of the church swung open, and all the dead entered, festively dressed, as was customary in the olden days; sweet music was played as they walked in and seated themselves in the pews. The psalm singing swelled like the rolling of the ocean. Jörgen's old foster parents from the Hunsby sand dunes were there, and the good Merchant Brönne and his wife, and beside them, next to Jörgen, sat their gentle, loving daughter. She gave her hand to Jörgen, and together they went up to the altar where they had knelt once before, and the pastor joined their hands and consecrated them to a life of love. Then the sound of the trumpet burst forth, marvelously like the voice of child, full of longing and expectation; it swelled into the sound of an organ, full of rich, glorious tones, blessed to hear and yet mighty enough to burst the tombstones on the graves.

The ship hanging in the choir sank downward, in front of them, and grew vast and splendid with silken sails and golden masts, with anchors of red gold and ropes of silken twine, like the ship in the old ballad. The bridal couple stepped on board, and all the congregation followed; there were room and enjoyment for all. Then the arches and walls of the church blossomed like the elder and the fragrant lime trees; joyfully they waved their green branches, and bowed, and parted. The ship was lifted up and sailed with them through the ocean, through the air. Every candle in the church became a tiny star; the winds sang a hymn, and all joined in:

"In love, to glory! No life shall be lost! Supreme happiness forever! Hallelujah!"

And these were Jörgen's last words in this mortal world, for the thread that held the immortal spirit snapped; only a lifeless corpse lay in the dark church, while the storm howled and covered it with drifting sand.

The next morning was Sunday, and the pastor and congregation set out for church. The road, buried in sand, was almost impassable. When they reached the church they found an enormous sand heap completely covering the door. Then the pastor prayed briefly and said that as God had now closed the door to this his house, they must go forth and raise Him a new one elsewhere. So they sang a psalm and returned home.

In vain Jörgen was sought throughout the town of Skagen and the sand dunes; it was supposed that the rolling waves of sand had buried him beneath them.

But his body was entombed in a vast sarcophagus, in the very church itself. During the storm our Lord cast earth over his coffin; the great heaps of sand lay above and around it, and they cover it to this day. The drifting sand lies piled above those mighty arches; thorns and wild roses now twine over the church, where the visitor struggles on toward its tower still showing above the sand. His tombstone may be seen for miles; no king ever had a more magnificent one. And no one will ever disturb the repose of the dead, for none until now has ever known his resting place; for this story was sung to me by the storm among the sand dunes.

MOVING DAY (1860)

You surely remember Ole, the tower watchman. I have told you about two visits I paid him, and now I'll tell you of a third, although it won't be the last one.

I have gone up to see him generally on New Year's Day, but this time it was Moving Day, when everything down in the city streets is very unpleasant, for they are littered with heaps of rubbish and crockery and all kinds of sweepings, not to mention musty old straw that you have to trample about in. Well, there I was, and in the middle of this rubbish from attic and dustbin I saw a couple of children playing going to bed; they thought it looked so inviting there for that game. Yes, they snuggled down in the straw and drew a ragged old scrap of a curtain over them for a quilt. "That was wonderful!" they said. It was too much for me, so I hurried off to see Ole.

"It's Moving Day," he said. "Streets and alleys are dustbins, dustbins in the grand style; but one cartload is enough for me. I can always find something to pick out of it, and I did that, soon after Christmas. I was walking down the street, a damp, raw, and dirty street, and just the right kind of weather for catching cold. The rubbish man had drawn up his cart there; it was loaded and looked like a sample of Copenhagen streets on Moving Day. In the back of the cart was a fir tree still quite green and with tinsel still hanging on its twigs. It had been the centerpiece of a Christmas display, but now it was thrown out into the street and the rubbish man had stuck it up behind on his pile; a sight to laugh at or weep at—yes, you might even go so far as that—it all depends on your turn of mind. And I thought about it, and so did some of the odds and ends in the cart. At least they may have thought, which is just about the same. Here was a worn lady's glove; what was it thinking about? Shall I tell you? It lay there pointing its little finger straight at the fir tree. 'That fir tree touches me,' it thought. 'I have been to a party, too, among the lighted chandeliers. My life was just a night at a ball. A squeeze of the hand, and I burst; that's all I remember, so now I have nothing more to live for.' That's the way the glove thought, or it may have thought like that. 'That's a tasteless thing for that fir tree to do!' said the potsherds. But you see, broken crockery finds everything tasteless. 'When you come to the rubbish cart,' they said, 'it's time to give up your fine airs and your tinsel. As for ourselves, we've been of some use in the world—far more use than an old green stick like that!' You see, that was another point of view on the same subject, and many people have it. But still the fir tree looked pretty well, and it was a bit of poetry on the rubbish heap; there are many like that to be found in the streets on Moving Day. But the streets down there were crowded and tiresome, and I longed to get back up to my tower and stay there; so here I sit and look down on them from above, and that's very amusing.

"Down below the good people are changing houses; they work hard packing up and then go off with their movables, and the house goblin sits on the tail of the cart and moves with them. Household quarrels, family arguments, sorrows, and cares move from the old to the new houses, and so what do they and we get out of it all? Yes, that was told us already long ago, in the good old verse in the newspaper columns:

Remember Death's Great Moving Day!

"It is a serious thought, but I hope it is not disagreeable to you to hear about it. Death is the most faithful administrator after all, in spite of his many petty duties. Have you ever thought about them?

"Death is a bus conductor; he is a passport writer; he signs his name to our references; and he is the director of life's great savings bank. Do you understand that? All our earthly deeds, great and small, are deposited in that savings bank. Then, when Death comes with his Moving Day bus and we have to get in to be driven to eternity, he gives us our references on the frontier as a passport. For our expense money on the journey he draws from the savings bank one of our deeds, whichever of them most distinctly characterizes our conduct; this may be very pleasant to us, or it may be very horrible!

"Nobody has ever escaped that omnibus journey. They tell stories, indeed, of one man who was not allowed to enter—they call him the Wandering Jew; he still has to run along behind it. If he had managed to get in, he would have escaped the treatment he received from the poets.

"Let's take an imaginary look into that big Moving Day omnibus. What a mixed group! Side by side sit kings and beggars, the genius and the idiot. On they must go, without goods or wealth, with only their references and their expense money from life's savings bank. But of each man's deeds, which one has been found and given to him? Perhaps only a very small one, no bigger than a pea, yet a great blooming vine may grow from it.

"The poor beggar, who sat on a low stool in the corner and

received blows and hard words, perhaps is given the battered stool to take, as a token and as expense money. That stool will become the cart to bear him into eternity, and there it will grow into a throne, gleaming with gold and blooming like an arbor.

"He who was always drinking from the bubbling cup of pleasure, and thus forgetting the wrong things he had done here, receives a wooden keg as his lot. On the journey he has to drink from it; and that pure and cleansing drink will clear his thoughts and awaken his better and nobler nature, so that he sees and feels what before he could not or would not see. Thus he bears within himself his own punishment, the gnawing worm that never dies. If on his wineglass was inscribed Forgetfulness, the inscription on the keg is Memory.

"Whenever I read a good historical book, I cannot help picturing to myself the person of whom I am reading at the final moment of all, when he begins to enter Death's omnibus. I cannot help wondering which of his deeds Death has given him from the savings bank, and what sort of expense money he will take with him to eternity.

"Once upon a time there was a French king—his name I have forgotten, for the names of good people can sometimes be forgotten by you and me, but it will surely come to light again, because in the time of famine this king became the savior of his people. In his honor they raised a monument of snow with the inscription, 'More quickly than this melts did you help us!' I think, remembering that monument, that Death must have given him one single snowflake that would never melt but flew like a white butterfly above his royal head, on into the land of eternity.

"Then there was Louis XI—yes, I remember his name; one always remembers what is wicked—a sample of his doings often comes to mind; I wish I could say the story is untrue.

"He had his lord high chancellor beheaded, and that he had a right to do, justly or unjustly; but on the same scaffold he set up the chancellor's innocent children, the one eight and the other seven, so that they would be spattered with their father's warm blood. Then they were taken to the Bastille and set in an iron cage, without even a blanket to cover them. Every eighth day the king sent the executioner to them, to pull a tooth from each of them, so that they might suffer even more. The elder said, 'My mother would die of sorrow if she knew how my little brother suffered. Pray, pull out two of my teeth, and spare him! There were tears in the hangman's eyes when he heard this, but the king's will was stronger than the tears. Every eighth day a silver dish, with two children's teeth on it, was brought to the king; as he had demanded them, so he had them. And I think it was two teeth that Death drew out of life's savings bank for Louis XI to take with him on his journey to the great land of eternity. They flew before him like two fireflies; they glowed and burned and stung him, the teeth of those innocent children."

"Yes, a serious drive it is, that bus drive on the great Moving Day. And when does our turn come?"

"That's why it's so very serious; any day, any hour, any minute the bus may come for us. Which of our deeds will Death draw from the savings bank and give us for the journey? Yes, think that over! That Moving Day will not be found on the calendar!"

THE BUTTERFLY (1860)

The Butterfly wanted a sweetheart, and naturally he wanted one of the prettiest of the dear little flowers. He looked at each of them; there they all sat on their stalks as quiet and modest as little maidens ought to sit before they are engaged; but there were so many to choose from that it would be quite difficult to decide. So the Butterfly flew down to the Daisy, whom the French call "Marguerite." They know she can tell fortunes. This is the way it's done: the lovers pluck off the little petals one by one, asking questions about each other, "Does he love me from the heart? A little? A lot? Or loves he not at all?"—or something like that; everyone asks in his own language. So the Butterfly also came to ask, but he wouldn't bite off the leaves; instead he kissed each one in turn, thinking that kindness is the best policy.

"Sweet Miss Marguerite Daisy," he said, "you're the wisest woman of all the flowers—you can tell fortunes! Tell me, should I choose this one or that one? Which one am I to have? When you have told me, I can fly straight to her and propose."

But Marguerite answered not a word. She resented his calling her "a woman," for she was unmarried and quite young. He put his question a second time, and then a third time, and when he still couldn't get a word out of her, he gave up and flew away to begin his wooing.

It was early spring; the snowdrops and crocuses were growing in abundance. "They're really very charming," said the Butterfly. "Neat little schoolgirls, but a bit too sweet." For, like all very young men, he preferred older girls. So he flew to the anemones, but they were a bit too bitter for his taste. The violets were a little too sentimental, the tulips much too gay, the lilies too middle class, the linden blossoms too small, and, besides, there were too many in their family. He admitted the apple blossoms looked like roses, but if they opened one day and the wind blew they fell to pieces the very next; surely such a marriage would be far too brief. He liked the sweet pea best of all; she was red and white, dainty and delicate, and belonged to that class of domestic girl who is pretty yet useful in the kitchen. He was about to propose to her when he noticed a pea pod hanging nearby, with a withered flower clinging to it. "Who's that?" he asked.

"It's my sister," said the pea flower.

"Oh, so that's how you'll look later on!" This frightened the Butterfly, and away he flew.

Honeysuckles hung over the hedges; there were plenty of those girls, long-faced and with yellow complexions. No, he didn't like that kind at all. Yes, but what did he like? You ask him!

Spring passed and summer passed; then autumn came, and he was still no nearer making up his mind. Now the flowers wore beautiful, colorful dresses, but what good did that do? The fresh, fragrant youth had passed, and it is fragrance the heart needs as one grows older; and of course dahlias and hollysocks have no particular fragrance. So the Butterfly went to see the mint.

"It's not exactly a flower—or rather it's all flower, fragrant from root to top, with sweet scent in every leaf. Yes, she's the one I want!" So at last he proposed to her.

But the mint stood stiff and silent, and at last said, "Friendship, if you like, but nothing else. I'm old, and you're old, too. It would be all right to live for each other, but marriage—no! Don't let's make fools of ourselves in our old age!"

And so the Butterfly did not find a sweetheart at all. He had hesitated too long, and one shouldn't do that! The Butterfly became an old bachelor, as we call it.

Now it was a windy and wet late autumn; the wind blew cold down the backs of the poor trembling old willows. And that made them creak all over. When the weather is like that it isn't pleasant to fly about in summer clothing, outside. But the Butterfly was not flying out-of-doors; he had happened to fly into a room where there was a fire in the stove and the air was as warm as summer. Here he could at least keep alive. "But just to keep alive isn't enough," he said. "To live you must have sunshine and freedom and a little flower to love!"

And he flew against the windowpane, was noticed by people, admired, and set on a needle to be stored in a butterfly collection. This was the most they could do for him.

"Now I'm sitting on a stalk, just like the flowers," said the Butterfly. "It isn't very much fun; it's just like being married, you're bound up so tightly!" He comforted himself with this reflection.

"A poor consolation, after all," said the pot plants in the room.

"But you can't take the opinion of pot plants," thought the Butterfly. "They converse too much with human beings!"

THE BISHOP OF BÖRGLUM AND HIS MEN (1861)

We are up in Jutland, near the wild marsh. We can hear the North Sea, hear it tossing about, for it is quite close by. Before us there rises a great sand dune; we have been looking at it for a long while, and we've been, and still are, driving toward it, very slowly, through the deep sand. On the top of this sand dune is an old, rambling building, the Börglum Monastery, the largest wing of which is the church. We arrive there in the late evening, but the air is clear and the night is bright, so we can enjoy an expansive view over meadow and moor as far as the Aalborg Fjord, over field and heath, out over the dark-blue sea.

Now that we are up there, we drive on through barn and shed, then turn through the gates and on into the old castle court, where the linden trees stand in a row along the walls; sheltered from wind and weather, they thrive here, and their leafy branches almost hide the windows.

We climb up the winding stone staircase; we then walk through the long corridors, beneath raftered ceilings. The wind whistles so strangely here, whether outside or inside; one doesn't quite know where the sounds come from. And then one tells stories. Yes, a person tells and sees so many things when he is frightened or wants to frighten others. The old dead monks, one says, glide silently past us and into the church, where the wind rushes through and seems to us to be singing Mass for their souls; this brings strange thoughts to one, thoughts that carry us back into the olden times.

There is a stranded ship on the coast, and the bishop's men are active there on the beach. While the ocean has spared some of the voyagers, these men spare none; the water will wash away all trace of crimson blood that has flowed from broken skulls. The stranded goods—and there are many—all belong to the bishop. The waves have washed up the anchor and barrels filled with fine wines for the cellar of the monks, where there is already a full supply of ale and mead; there is also a plenitude of poultry, sausages, and ham in their kitchen, and in the ponds outside are fat bass and delicious carp. The Bishop of Börglum is a man of power; he owns much land and yet he wants to acquire more; all must bow before him, Oluf Glob. A wealthy kinsman of his, at Thy, has just died; the widow will find Oluf Glob neither kin nor kind to her. Her late husband ruled the whole district, with the exception of the church properties; her son is in a foreign land, having been sent away, at his own wish, when no more than a boy, to learn foreign customs. For years no word has come from him; he may be in his grave and may never return home to take over the rule that now his mother must assume.

"What! Shall a woman rule?" says the bishop. He summons her into the courts, but for what gain? She has broken no law; right and justice are on her side.

Bishop Oluf of Börglum, what are you pondering over? What are you writing on that white parchment? What is it that you now conceal under band and seal and then give to a knight and his servant, who ride off with it, out of the country, far away to the city of the pope?

The time of the falling leaves, the season of storms and

wrecks, is past, and now icy winter comes. Twice it has come with no tidings from abroad, but now finally with its return the knight and his servant ride back from Rome, bearing a papal ban against the widow who dared oppose the pious bishop.

"A curse upon her and all that is hers! Cast out is she from church and congregation. None shall dare lend her a helping hand; friends and kinfolk alike must shun her as a plague and pestilence! What will not bend must break," said the bishop.

The people all forsake her; yet she is steadfast in her trust in God, who alone will be her strength and bulwark. Only one servant, an elderly maid, remains faithful to her; together they guide the plow over fields where the corn flourishes, though the land has been cursed.

"You child of hell, I shall yet carry out my purpose!" says the Bishop of Börglum. "Now I summon you before the tribunal that will condemn you!"

Then the widow harnesses her last two oxen to her carriage, and she and her faithful servant drive away across the heath, out of the land of Denmark. Now she is a stranger among strangers, where a strange tongue is spoken, and where foreign customs prevail, far away, where the green hills rise into mountains, and where the vineyards grow. Traveling peddlers pass her, carefully guarding their loaded wagons, in deadly fear of attack from robber barons. But the two poor women, in their humble cart drawn by the black oxen, may pass in safety along the dangerous roads and through the dense forests. Now they are in France, and they meet a gallant knight followed by twelve men-at-arms. The knight pauses and looks at the strange wagon and then asks the younger of the women what country they have come from and what their journey's destination is. She explains that they are from Thy, in Denmark, tells of her cares and misery, but these all seem to come to an end; our Lord has guided them together—the stranger knight is her son! He holds out his arms and embraces her, and the poor mother weeps, which she has not been able to do for many years, but rather has bitten her lips until blood has come forth.

It is the time of the falling leaves, the season of wrecks. The ocean washes ashore filled wine casks for the bishop's cellars; in his kitchen the wild venison is roasting; it is pleasant and warm within doors, though winter freezes without. But news is brought; Jens Glob has returned to Thy with his mother. Jens Glob summons the bishop into court to demand their lands and rights.

"Much good that will do him!" said the bishop. "Spare your efforts, Sir Jens!"

Another year passes; again the time of the falling leaves returns, the season of wrecks; icy winter follows, and the white bees swarm about and sting one's face until they melt. It is sharp weather today, say people who have ventured out into it. Jens Glob stands close to his fire, lost in thought; he singes his mantle, burns a hole in it unawares. "I will master you yet, Bishop of Börglum! You are safe from the law, sheltered by the mantle of the Pope, but not safe from Jens Glob!" He writes to his brother-in-law, Sir Oluf Hase of Salling, bidding him meet him Christmas Eve at Mass in Hvidberg Church; the bishop must leave Börglum and come to Thyland, to read the Mass there; this Jens Glob knows.

Meadow and moorland are buried beneath ice and snow, and across them speeds a cavalcade of horse and riders—the bishop, his clerks, his squires. They take the short cut among the waving reeds, where the wind sings its melancholy song. Blow your brazen trumpet, you trumpeter dressed in foxskin! It sounds sharply in the clear air! They ride on over heath and moorland, where in the warm summertime Fata Morgana decks her magic bowers; on they ride, to the south, toward Hvidberg Church.

The wind blows his trumpet, too, blows it louder and louder, creating a storm, a terrible storm, that continues to grow in force. On, on through the storm, toward the church, they ride. The house of God stands firm, but the storm drives on over field and moorland, over fjord and ocean. The bishop reaches the church. But Sir Oluf Hase can scarcely do so, however hard he rides. He reaches the opposite side of the fjord with his men, whom Jens Glob has summoned to aid him in calling the bishop to account. The church is the courthouse; the altar is the counsel table. The candles in the heavy brass candlesticks are all burning. Outside the storm screams out the accusation and the sentence. The wind rushes through the air, over moorland and heath, over the rolling billows; no ferryboat can cross the fjord in such weather.

Oluf Hase is held at Ottesund; he dismisses his men, bids them keep his horse and armor and take his farewell to his wife, for alone will he risk his life in the roaring waters. They will be his witnesses that it is not his fault if Jens Glob stands alone in Hvidberg Church. But his faithful warriors will not leave him; they will follow him even into the raging waters. Ten of them are swept away by the torrent; Oluf Hase and the two youngest reach the opposite shore in safety and have still four miles to ride.

It is past midnight, Christmas Eve. The wind has died down; the church is lighted up, the light shining from the windows over meadow and heath. The service is ended, and the house of God is so still that the wax can be heard dripping from the candles to the stone floor. Now at last Oluf Hase arrives.

Jens Glob meets him in the forecourt, saying, "Good day. The bishop and I are reconciled now!"

"Are you, indeed!" says Oluf. "Then neither you nor the bishop shall leave this church alive!" His sword flashes from its scabbard and splits in two the wooden door of the church, which Jens has closed between them. "Hold back, dear brother-in-law! First see what sort of reconciliation this is! I have slain the bishop and all his men! Not one of them will do evil again, and we need say nothing more of the wrongs done my mother!"

The altar lights burn red, but redder is the stain that shines from the church door; there, lying in blood, is the bishop, with a cloven skull, and lying dead around him are his men. It is quiet and calm on the holy eve of Christmas.

The third evening after Christmas, funeral bells in Börglum Convent. The murdered bishop and his slain men lie in state beneath a black canopy, lighted by candelabras swathed in crepe. The once mighty lord is a corpse, robed in a silver-bordered mantle, with the crosier in his powerless hand. Incense fills the air as the monks chant a funeral dirge; it sounds like a sentence of wrath and condemnation, and may be heard over the whole countryside as it is carried along and wailed by the wind. Sometimes the accusing voice sinks to rest for a while, but it never dies out completely; it always rises again, carrying its dismal strains late into our own century, singing of the cruel Bishop of Börglum and his wicked men. On many a dark night the terrified peasant, driving along the heavy sandy road past Börglum Convent, hears it; and the sleepless listener within Börglum's thick walls hears it, too. The church entrance has long been walled up, but superstitious eyes still see the door there, opening before them; the candles in the church brass crowns shine, and the church is revealed in its former splendor, rich with the smoke of incense, while the monks still sing the funeral Mass for the murdered bishop. He lies there in his silver-bordered robe, the crosier in his powerless hand, the bloody wound shining as red as fire from his pale, proud forehead. There are the worldly mind and evil passions that burned.

Sink into the grave, into the night of oblivion, you dismal memories of the olden days!

Listen to the voice of the wind, sweeping over the rolling sea! Out there a storm is raging and will take many lives, for the sea has not changed its nature because the times have changed. Tonight it is all mouths to devour; tomorrow perhaps it will be as clear as a mirror, just as it was in the olden times we have now buried. Sleep calmly if you can!

Now it is morning; the new day brings sunshine into the room. But the wind still blows, and there is news of a wreck, as in the olden times. Last night, down by Lökken, the little red-roofed fishing village visible from our windows, a ship was wrecked. But by the use of a rocket apparatus a line was cast ashore and a bridge made between the wreck and the mainland; all on board were saved and brought to land, and beds were found for them. Today they are going to Börglum Convent. There they will find warm hospitality, be sheltered in comfortable rooms, see friendly eyes, and hear kindly voices speaking their own language. The piano will sound for them with melodies of their native land, and before these have died away, a chord of another sort will be struck; soundless and yet full of sound and certainty, the telegraph wire will reach the homes of the shipwrecked in a foreign land and tell of their safety. Then with their minds at ease, they will join in the dancing at the feast given in the hall at Börglum. Waltzes and folk dances will be danced, and songs will be sung about Denmark and her valiant soldier in our time.

Blessed be you, our new age! Let a fresh and pure summer breeze sweep through the towns! Send your sunrays into our hearts and minds! Let them erase the dark traditions of the cruel days of old!